THE

INFLUENTIAL

Woman

VICKIE KRAFT

WORD PUBLISHING
Dallas·London·Vancouver·Melbourne

Library of Congress Cataloging-in-Publication Data:

Kraft, Vickie.
    The influential woman : how every woman can make a dynamic difference in other women's lives / Vickie Kraft.
       p.   cm.
    Includes index.
    ISBN 0–8499–3349–8
    1. Women—Religious life.   2. Women—Conduct of life.
I. Title.
BV4527.K7234   1992
248.8'43—dc20   92–8865
                                                 CIP

   49 LB 9 8 7 6 5 4 3
Printed in the United States of America

To Fred, my husband

with love and thanks for his
encouragement and support

Contents

Acknowledgments

Many people have contributed to this book. I appreciate the thousands of women who have shared their lives with me during the Bible classes, retreats, and seminars conducted through Titus 2:4 Ministries, Inc. Some of their stories are included here, but the names and details have been changed to protect their identities.

I am grateful for the women of Northwest Bible Church in Dallas, Texas, who requested a structure to provide for meaningful relationships between older and younger women and then worked to implement and refine it.

I am indebted to Dr. James C. Dobson, whose interview with us on the "Focus on the Family" radio program gave nationwide exposure to the Heart-to-Heart ministry. These broadcasts drew thousands of responses from women all over the country.

Two women in my family have my sincere gratitude for their critiquing of the manuscript: my daughter, Helene Kraft Cronin, who read the material with discernment and contributed valuable insight; and my cousin, Grace Watkins, who made constructive suggestions.

Nancy Norris, my editor at Word Publishing, has my warm thanks for her personal encouragement and her professional handling of this entire project.

Finally, Lela Gilbert has my heartfelt appreciation for her careful editing and her sensitive input.

Vickie Kraft

1

Why Women Need Women

*D*iane was flooded with joy as she looked down at the newborn son in her arms. Feeling almost triumphant, she rode down the hospital hall in a wheelchair, headed for home. Just five days before, little Todd had been delivered by Caesarean section, and although Diane's spirits were strong, her legs were not. She was grateful not to be walking all the way to the parking lot.

Her husband Gordon pulled the car up to the curb, and gingerly strapped the baby into the infant carrier. Settling in for the ride, Diane felt a wave of fatigue.

"I'm sure glad you're taking the week off to help me, Honey. I don't think I could have managed both babies without you. I just hope Terry doesn't feel too jealous of Todd."

Two-year-old Terry, their other son, was awaiting their arrival at the next-door neighbors' house. As Diane turned to smile at the sleeping infant in the back seat, she caught her breath in pain. She was still very sore.

Gordon cleared his throat. "Uh, Honey, I need to talk to you about taking the week off."

She stared at her husband. Surely he wasn't going to let her down now. Not this time!

"Talk about what?"

"Well, you know it's end-of-the-month, and John doesn't think he can spare me at the office. I kept saying no, I had to help you. But he finally talked me into working when he offered to pay for a maid to help you."

Tears filled Diane's eyes. She looked out the side window, not wanting Gordon to know how wounded she felt. It wasn't just the fact that she needed her husband's help, although she needed it very badly. Didn't he want to take care of her?

"Well, are you upset or what?" Her silence annoyed Gordon and he sounded defensive.

"I . . . I'm just disappointed. Gordon, I have no idea where to find a maid. Nobody we know even has a cleaning lady. And I wouldn't know where to begin looking for someone I could trust with my babies. Besides, I thought you'd want to be there with Todd and me . . ."

"Well, look. If I don't do things John's way, I won't have a job, and we won't even be able to feed Todd and Terry. Besides, you're tough. You can handle it."

Diane looked out the window again. *I am tough,* she thought. *I've had to be.*

Things went better than she'd hoped when Terry ran across the lawn to greet her. How she'd missed him at the hospital! The little brown-eyed toddler had been her pride and joy every day for two wonderful years.

"Come meet your new brother!"

Terry ran to her arms and then surveyed the little bundle in the car seat. "Baby?" he said inquisitively. He spontaneously reached over and touched Todd's face. "Baby," he said to himself, quite satisfied with his conclusion.

She took Terry in her arms, saddened that she couldn't pick him up—her stitches wouldn't permit it. She had always carried him. Would he feel neglected now if she didn't?

"I'm taking the rest of the afternoon off," Gordon announced generously, "so I can help you out."

Next morning Diane was exhausted—she'd been up since five o'clock. Todd had nursed every two hours all night, and

Terry had awakened her twice while Todd slept. Gordon hadn't heard a thing and had left for work at seven o'clock. Fatigue made her limbs ache. At eight, the phone began to ring, well-meaning friends calling in their congratulations.

"I'm hungry," Terry informed her, and she slowly shuffled into the kitchen to feed him. Another phone call interrupted her, and while she was talking, the little boy opened the refrigerator and knocked a full carton of milk and a half-eaten pie onto the floor. Diane couldn't bend over, and the mop wasn't particularly effective in cleaning up the pie.

Ants. I'm going to have a million ants . . .

Just then Todd started to cry.

"Baby cry!" Terry proclaimed, running toward the nursery.

"No, Terry! Don't touch him!" Diane rushed—too fast— to keep Terry from trying to pick up the now-squalling infant. Breast milk suddenly soaked the front of her robe.

She picked up Todd, sank heavily onto the bed, and began to nurse him, feeling dizzy and shaky. Fear rippled through her. *What if I pass out? I won't. I just can't!*

Terry watched his little brother nurse and tugged at Diane's robe. It hadn't been all that long since she'd weaned him, and he somehow felt hurt by his new brother's closeness to her.

Tears for Terry stung her eyes. She loved him so dearly, and he was too little to understand the intrusion of a new baby. Diane's tears were for herself, too, because she felt abandoned by her husband. She wasn't really angry—it was her nature to make excuses for his negligence. But she was hurt, and her pain was acute, aggravated by exhaustion and surging postpartum hormones.

She gradually began to weep, deeply and sorrowfully.

"Mommy cry! Mommy cry!" Terry looked at her in dismay and patted her arm. It made her feel ten times worse.

"God, help me . . ."

Her eyes fell on the phone, which hadn't rung for all of fifteen minutes. As much as she hated to admit it, she needed help. But who could she call?

She tried to focus her weary mind on her list of friends. Everyone she could think of was either at work or had little ones at home. Then she remembered Laurie Hawkins.

Laurie was a woman at their church who had been linked with her through an innovative program called Heart-to-Heart. The two women had committed themselves to a supportive Christian friendship, and talked and prayed regularly, usually by phone. Laurie was twenty years older than Diane, and had raised several children of her own. She'd called the hospital once, and Diane vaguely recalled her having said something like, "Let me know if you need anything."

She's probably going to wish she hadn't offered . . . but here goes. Balancing Todd against her breast, Diane tried to remember the number which she should have known by heart. Her mind was blank. She fumbled through the H's in the church directory until she found the right number. Terry began to scream, as he often did, when she picked up the receiver.

"Shh!" she frowned at him. It was all she could do to hear the friendly "Hello" on the other end of the line.

"Laurie? It's Diane." Terry's wails continued.

"Well, hello! You're home! How are you doing there? Sounds like you've got your hands full."

"Oh, I'm fine. I just . . ." Unexpectedly, Diane's voice broke. "I guess I need some help," she whispered.

"I'll be right over."

Laurie was at the door in less than an hour. Her arms were filled with groceries, videos for Terry to watch, and a stuffed animal for him to play with. "I didn't bring anything for the baby. He doesn't know the difference right now anyway, and this little guy needs all the attention he can get!"

Diane began to cry again, this time with relief and gratitude. She explained the entire situation to the older woman, and even managed to express her disappointment with Gordon.

"I can understand your feelings, Diane, and I know it's not the first time this kind of thing has happened. But for now just forgive him. Gordon loves you, and he thinks he's doing the best for you by pleasing his boss and keeping his job secure. That's the way men think. You can talk it over with him later when you're stronger. But go lie down now, while Todd's asleep. You'll feel better when you wake up."

When Diane awoke, the house was orderly, fresh laundry was in the dryer, Terry was happily watching cartoons, and Todd was in Laurie's arms quietly sucking on a pacifier. "I can never thank you enough, Laurie."

"Well, don't thank me yet—I still want to make dinner. Listen, Diane, if it's all right with you, I'm going to come over for the next few days. Frankly, I think you're going to need help for at least a week."

A Heartfelt Cry

Yes, women need women. And as demonstrated by Diane's story, our own church in Dallas, Texas, has successfully launched a formal program called Heart-to-Heart, which links women into relationships for prayer, encouragement, emotional support, and friendship. In our particular situation, we place senior/junior partners together for a year's time. The two agree to meet together at least once a month and to speak to each other by phone no less than once a week. They are "officially" committed to one another for this period of time, but their friendships usually last far longer. (For more information about Heart-to-Heart, please see the Appendix.)

Not long ago, after speaking at a women's retreat, I received a note.

> I am thirty-four years old, the wife of a policeman who works rotating shifts, the mother of three children, two in school and one in preschool. I am very excited about what you have been teaching us. I found myself choking back tears the whole time, because you were addressing so many things relevant to my life. I would so love to have an older godly Christian woman teach me! You are right on target when you say there aren't

support groups for one another anymore. People are all working outside the home and those of us who feel called to be at home suffer with isolation and loneliness.

Everywhere I go, I hear the same cry from women—young and old, rich and poor, married and single. "I'm lonely. I'm tired. I'm discouraged and depressed. My husband just doesn't understand my needs. My mother isn't there for me. Does anybody care? Will anybody help me, or even listen to me?"

Now, more than ever, godly women should be reaching out, stepping out, and speaking out. In today's world we're being confronted with challenges never before faced by any generation. Dramatic social changes. An astronomically high divorce rate. A large percentage of mothers working outside the home. Materialism that has deceived us into thinking that "things" are more important than people. The media-inspired concept that only career women are fulfilling themselves as individuals. All of this has contributed to unrest, dissatisfaction, and confusion.

Feminists with a humanistic world-view have been talking about women's concerns for years. On some points we can agree with them. Self-esteem is not derived from our connection to a man. We know that it is not found in raising children successfully, nor is it the by-product of career success or material wealth. But Christian women have more than an "inner self" to provide us with personal guidance and satisfaction. Christians have access to Someone beyond ourselves, giving us unlimited power and resources, and matchless hope for the future.

As women of God, our self-esteem lies in the immense value God, our Creator, has placed upon and within us.

Our Creator has not only given us a priceless position in His creation, He has also provided us with clear instruction as to our proper place in other women's lives. Whether we involve ourselves in formal programs, such as Heart-to-Heart (which, by the way, I highly recommend), or we simply choose to care for those in our circle of acquaintances informally, we have a wonderful biblical mandate for such relationships. God's Word promises every Christian woman strength, direction, and support, not only for herself, but for those she wants to help.

Wise Advice to a Young Pastor

Women helping women is not a new idea at all. It was initiated in the Christian church some two thousand years ago. In the first century Paul the Apostle sent a letter to a young pastor named Titus, whom he had dispatched to the Island of Crete. Titus' job was to help the young church there grow to maturity. Titus faced two major problems. Those new believers had been raised in a pagan society, and a very immoral one at that. To further complicate matters, he was also competing with false teachers who were deceiving and confusing the new converts.

Of course, we still have those same problems today. In our western civilization, Christianity is losing its influence and its power because many times there is little discernible difference between the Christian and the non-Christian. Many people who turn to Christ come out of either pagan or distorted religious backgrounds. They don't know what a godly mother, wife, father, husband, son, or daughter should be like. It's almost unnecessary to mention the false teaching that is spewed out of the media, our educational institutions, and even some of our pulpits. Each generation of new believers has to see the Christian life lived out before them by godly role models who are committed to God's Word as their standard for truth. Paul's advice to Titus is as relevant and workable today as it was then.

> You must teach what is in accord with sound doctrine. Teach the older men to be temperate, worthy of respect, self-controlled, and sound in faith, in love and in endurance.
> Likewise, teach the older women to be reverent in the way they live, not to be slanderers or addicted to much wine,

but to teach what is good. Then they can train the younger women to love their husbands and children, to be self-controlled and pure, to be busy at home, to be kind, and to be subject to their husbands, so that no one will malign the word of God.

Similarly, encourage the young men to be self-controlled. In everything set them an example by doing what is good. In your teaching show integrity, seriousness and soundness of speech that cannot be condemned, so that those who oppose you may be ashamed because they have nothing bad to say about us.

Titus 2:1–8

Qualified by God

Just for the record, let's assure ourselves that women who reach out to women don't have to be graduates of colleges, universities, seminaries, or Bible schools. You may not have a degree from anywhere. But you do have something that is much more important. You have lived!

You have experienced life. You've rejoiced in birth and faced the reality of death. You may be a mother. You may have a career. You may be widowed. You may have been through divorce. You may be single, never married. You may have come through times of great failure and repentance. No matter where life has taken you, you have gone through all kinds of joy and suffering and you have something to share.

Why? Because in spite of all you've been through, you have not become embittered toward God. Instead you've walked with Him. You've let Him minister to you. You have not turned away, but have instead grown closer to Him. And now you have something to offer others who are in the very same boat.

You have been equipped for this responsibility in another important way. God has given spiritual gifts to every one of His children, including His daughters. And those gifts were not meant to confine you to making cookies or working in the church nursery! There is much, much more here for you to do.

Furthermore, you are responsible to use your gifts. They are not "optional equipment."

Why do you think God wants women to reach out to women?

Well, for one thing, we can do it better than anyone else. I say this without any apology whatsoever. Only a woman knows what it's like to go through a difficult pregnancy. To suffer PMS or postpartum blues. To work through the terrible fatigue that results from chasing toddlers for hours on end. Only a woman can relate to the boredom and isolation of speaking to children all day in monosyllables. Only a woman understands the subtle (and sometimes not-so-subtle) discrimination sometimes confronted both at work and at church. Only a woman can really understand how another woman feels.

And only a woman can follow up properly. It's easy for us to call each other and ask, "How did the talk with your husband go yesterday?" "Are you feeling better?" "Why don't you come over for coffee? We can talk a little more and pray together."

This type of loving concern and practical advice often will defuse conflicts before they reach a crisis stage that threatens the marriage or requires long-term professional counseling.

Probably the most obvious reason for older women to counsel and train younger women is that it helps avoid the opportunity for temptation. There are some rather grim statistics regarding immorality within the Christian church. A high percentage of these tragic circumstances originates when men take the job God ordained for women—the long-term counseling of younger women. Women should be doing the job they were called to do!

Getting Ready to Reach Out

Is every woman eligible to minister to others? No. In fact, Paul specifies some guidelines for eligibility. In the first place it goes without saying that, within a Christian context, the woman who wishes to involve herself in the lives of others must be a believer in the Lord Jesus Christ. She is to be reverent in the way she lives. Now that doesn't mean she sprouts a halo and keeps her hands in a holy, prayerful position while she goes about her daily chores. In the original language in which the Bible was written, the word translated "reverent" described a priestess serving in the temple of her God. For us, then, it means that she sees the world as a temple, and herself as God's servant within it.

That perspective removes any sacred/secular division from our lives. It isn't any more spiritual for you to teach a Sunday school class than it is for you to prepare nutritious meals for your family. It's no holier for you to sing in the church choir than it is for you to be a responsible secretary, full of integrity. Work, whatever it is, is not something that you leave behind in order to pursue ministry. For the believer, all of life is sacred, and every act is an act of ministry (1 Cor. 10:31).

In his letter to Titus, Paul goes on to say that the woman who ministers to other women should not be a slanderer. If women are going to trust you with their heartbreaks, you'd better not be a gossip! You must be able to keep a confidence. You must be trustworthy.

Nor are we to be addicts. Now, the Scripture actually says, "Nor addicted to much wine," and it was specifically speaking of drunkards. But I think we can take that warning a little further. Addiction to external substances or activities—drugs, alcohol, soap operas, food, even shopping—is an escape from our secret pain. We need to learn to handle life by placing our dependence on the Lord. Otherwise we don't have much to offer others.

Finally, this older or more mature woman is to be "a teacher of what is good."

There is a presupposition in all this—something we must know in order to carry out our responsibilities to each other. We must know the Word of God. We've got to know what the Bible teaches—not only what it states specifically, but what it expresses in principle. And that is, in large part, what this book is about. What does the Bible say to us as women? Who are we in God's great design? How does He want us to live, to enjoy life, to fulfill ourselves? And what are the concepts we are to teach our women friends?

Sharing Invaluable Lessons

Certainly we are all still working through our own learning process. We always will be. As we find our way, with God's help, through our own times of difficulty and darkness, we are able to offer our deeper understanding to those we love.

One of the lessons Titus 2 teaches us is to be "husband lovers." As we develop healthy relationships between ourselves and our husbands, we incorporate such qualities as friendship, pleasure, and enjoyment.

Young women, especially newlyweds, need us to teach them patience and wisdom. A lot of us have acquired these qualities through hard experience, but that isn't necessarily the best way to learn. I am amazed at how much help is received when one woman explains to another the basic differences between men and women.

Not so long ago, a young woman stormed into my office. She was an attractive twenty-year-old, but her face was clouded with frustration. "You wouldn't believe how disappointed I am in my husband!" She took a deep breath and shook her head. "You know we've been married less than a year, right? Well, he's just about stopped talking to me! I'm so upset . . ."

"What happens when you try to talk to him?"

Her answer was just what I thought it would be. "Oh, he's either watching the news, listening to the stereo, messing around with his computer—whatever. Everything seems more important than what I have to say. He mumbles one or two words, and that's it!"

I couldn't help but smile, "You know, Carole, that's really fairly typical of men."

A frown of disbelief creased her forehead. "It's typical? You mean it isn't just him? He makes me feel like I'm the most boring woman in the world!"

Much has been written about male-female communication. Norman Wright has addressed this issue with particular insight in his books on communication. He points out that women amplify and men condense. You know what I mean, don't you? You're desperately trying to tell the man in your life the whole story including all the details. He says, "Get to the bottom line! What happened?"

Or, he comes home from work and tells you the bottom line.

You immediately want to know, "But what happened to begin with?"

He looks at you with frustration. "I just told you, didn't I?"

There are a number of other basic differences between men and women. Most women are relational; most men are analytical. Face it, some surveys indicate that less than 10 percent of the men in America have one personal friend. Did you think it was just your husband who didn't have any friends? As we are learning to love our husbands—to enjoy and appreciate them and, yes, to be their friends, we can teach other wives to do the same.

We can also help women to be "children lovers." This is a hostile world for children. If they are not murdered in the womb, they risk neglect, abuse, molestation, and incest. It is important for us to try to encourage young mothers to stay home whenever possible and to take care of their own small children. Young mothers need older "veterans" to give them perspective and hope. Sometimes just saying, "This too will pass!" can help a mom get through another exhausting day.

Paul also pointed out that older women need to teach younger women to have self-control. That word doesn't mean just abstaining from impulses. It means to make someone sane! It also means to be discreet. To be sensible. To be unafraid of the future. It means to yield to the Holy Spirit's control.

How on earth are we going to teach those lessons? By example. By transparency. By humbly sharing how we've had to learn some tough lessons ourselves. This means that we have to be open, honest, and vulnerable. The women we share our lives with have to see that we understand because we've "been there."

Prayer, Purity, and Wise Words

I think it's wonderful for women to take the opportunity to pray together. I don't know how many times I have been in my kitchen making a meal while talking on the telephone to a friend about a personal problem.

One of us will say, "Let's pray right now."

Without taking any time away from our responsibilities, we've prayed together right then and there. Within a matter of days, my friends and I have recounted to each other how God mightily used that one quick moment of prayer to change the course of circumstances. And it's just that much better to actually sit together and pray at length about mutual needs, dreams, and difficulties.

Women are best equipped to teach other women about sexual purity—chastity before marriage and fidelity after. Purity implies being a "one-man woman." We need biblical truths to counteract our contemporary culture. Marriage is supposed to be a commitment without alternative. And in this day, when even Christians are engaging in immorality and are embroiled in divorces, we especially need to deal with this very essential and sensitive subject.

And isn't it delightful that we have the opportunity to share with other women helpful suggestions about home management? One of my favorite verses is 1 Timothy 5:14. It says that the woman is to be the manager of the home. (The Greek word literally means "house despot"!) Unfortunately, there is such an overemphasis on marital submission in some circles that many women feel more like a servant than a queen. In the home, a woman is not only responsible, but she is also authoritative. She manages the house (not her husband), and expresses her creativity and skills while providing a safe haven for her family. These accomplishments are bound to give her a great sense of satisfaction.

Paul also advises us to teach each other to be subject to our own husbands. This has been mistaught, overtaught, and often taught in such an unbalanced way that most women flinch inwardly when they hear it. I believe we are going to make some surprising discoveries when we come to that chapter. (See chapter 5, The Truth About Submission.)

For example, did you know that biblical submission is voluntary submission to the leadership of your husband? You submit because you are obedient to Jesus Christ, not because God or your husband compels you to. By His design, you and your husband are a leadership team of equals, and he simply has the final word. This is not just his privilege—it is his responsibility. Furthermore, it doesn't imply submission to all men by all women. And it most certainly does not mean, in any sense, that women are inferior.

Why is the role of women so important to God? What is the purpose of our teaching and caring for each other? Paul explained it by saying: "So that no one will malign the word of God." The Phillips paraphrase of the New Testament puts it this way, "So that we will be a good advertisement for the Christian faith."

In the first century a Roman writer enviously commented, "What women these Christians have!" It was obvious they were different. Proverbs 31 describes a godly woman who was honored by her husband, by her children, and by the community. When you and I live the kind of life God intended for us, it's going to make an impact on others. Each of us has a circle of influence that we can powerfully impact when we are the kind of women God wants us to be.

It all sounds great, doesn't it? Women helping women; women understanding women; women having a great deal of influence in the lives of others. But how can we apply all this to our daily lives? First of all, we must be available to each other. Let's try not to get our schedules so full or so inflexible that there is no time for people. I get really concerned when someone says, "I wanted to call you all week but I didn't. I know how busy you are!" I hope I'm never too busy to care.

Ruth and Naomi—A Life-Changing Love

Additionally, once we've decided to get involved with others, we must seek God's counsel and direction. There is a story in the Bible that will demonstrate how beautifully one woman can make a transformative difference in the life of another. The Old Testament book of Ruth is an exciting, wonderful narrative with special meaning to women helping women. We can particularly apply it to relationships between older and younger women, but it speaks encouragement to us all.

Naomi and Ruth shared what we call a *symbiotic* relationship. A *parasitic* relationship occurs when one person does all the giving and the other does all the taking. A symbiotic relationship is one that is mutually beneficial.

The story of Ruth, in its historical setting, is a diamond sparkling on black velvet. It was written when the Hebrews were ruled by judges, and there was no king. Judges 21:25 comments that in those days "everyone did as he saw fit." We have a society much like that today. Unfortunately, when people do what is right in their own eyes, it often turns out to be wrong.

So it's no surprise that we read in verse 1 of Ruth, "In the days when the judges ruled, there was famine in the land." In the Old Testament famines were usually intended to bring people back to God. We read:

> There was a famine in the land, and a man from Bethlehem in Judah, together with his wife and two sons, went to live for a while in the country of Moab. The man's

name was Elimelech, his wife's name Naomi, and the names of his two sons were Mahlon and Kilion. They were Ephrathites from Bethlehem, Judah. And they went to Moab and lived there.

Ruth 1:1–2

After ten years, Elimelech, Naomi's husband, and her two sons died. Naomi had lost everything—except for the two Moabite women her sons had married. In all the darkness, Naomi and her daughters-in-law finally saw a little spark of hope. They heard that the Lord had come to the aid of His people, and the famine was over in Israel. Upon hearing this news, Naomi made the decision to go back to Bethlehem. Orpah and Ruth decided to join her.

Naomi must have been a wonderful mother-in-law, considering that those two women wanted to leave their own society, their own home, their own background—everything they knew that was familiar—and were willing to go with her.

It was the custom regarding widows in that day that their deceased husband's brothers or other near-relatives in the family were responsible for them. Naomi said to her daughters-in-law, "I don't have any more sons, girls, so you'd better not come back with me."

Making the Right Choices

In so many words, she released them. She was willing to give up their companionship rather than deprive them of the opportunity to find other husbands. She was unselfishly concerned about them. She knew she would be abandoned and lonely, but she put their interests first.

I think this is an important principle. When we are ministering to other people, we must not be self-seeking. We should always consider the other person's interests and needs rather than our own. Older women whose kids have left the nest often yearn to feel they are needed. Sometimes they inadvertently become demanding and possessive of their young friends.

Naomi was not only unselfish, she was also encouraging when she said, "May the Lord show kindness to you, as you have shown to your dead and to me" (Ruth 1:8). She was saying they had been good wives. Women who reach out to others must be upbeat, encouraging, and supportive. They should help their friends find their strengths, while not obligating them.

After Naomi released the girls, "They wept again. Then Orpah kissed her mother-in-law good-bye, but Ruth clung to her."

Orpah made a logical decision. She decided to go back home to Moab to look for a new husband there. This is the last we hear of Orpah—she walks off the pages of history.

But Ruth made a different choice. "Look," said Naomi, "your sister-in-law is going back to her people and her gods. Go back with her."

Ruth replied,

> Don't urge me to leave you or to turn back from you. Where you go I will go, and where you stay I will stay. Your people will be my people and your God my God. Where you die I will die, and there I will be buried. May the Lord deal with me, be it ever so severely, if anything but death separates you and me.

> Ruth 1:16–17

In these beautiful words Ruth convinced Naomi of her love and commitment. Naomi's people and God would be hers, too. She even took an oath. Ruth was determined to stay under a godly influence, with no material benefits, rather than go back to Moab and its false gods.

Just as Naomi respected Ruth's decision, we shouldn't impose our opinions upon our younger friends. It's our role to explain the possible consequences of their actions, then to allow them to make choices. We are not to take authority over others, but rather to serve as advisers. This is very important, especially in older/younger relationships. The elder is not the boss. She has not acquired a new child. She is a guide, a mentor, an adult advising an adult.

Each One Helping the Other

When they finally arrived back in Bethlehem, the women there were shocked by Naomi's changed appearance and lamentable circumstances. "Can this be Naomi?" they said.

"Don't call me Naomi," she told them. "Call me Mara, because the Almighty has made my life very bitter. I went away full, but the Lord has brought me back empty." God did bring Naomi back empty, but we are about to see Him fill her again—because of her relationship with Ruth.

Naomi returned from Moab with Ruth just as the barley harvest was beginning, a time of hope and anticipation. But that's not what Naomi was feeling. She said, "The Lord has afflicted me; the Almighty has brought misfortune upon me." She was depressed and in despair.

> And Ruth the Moabitess said to Naomi, "Let me go to the fields and pick up the leftover grain behind anyone in whose eyes I find favor."
>
> Ruth 2:2

Now we begin to see the mutual benefits of this relationship.

Naomi said to her "Go ahead, my daughter." Ruth is strong and young and Naomi has been weakened by passing years and a heavy heart. Ruth sees that it will be her responsibility to provide for them both. And she does so without any hesitation. She loves Naomi and she wants to do her part in providing for their livelihood. So she says, "I will glean."

As it turned out, she found herself gleaning on a property belonging to Boaz, a man who was from the clan of Naomi's husband Elimelech. Naturally, for people of faith, "As it turned out . . ." never describes coincidence. It indicates God's leading.

When Boaz arrived from Bethlehem he asked the foreman of his harvesters, "Whose young woman is that?"

The foreman replied, "She is the Moabitess who came back from Moab with Naomi. . . . She went into the field and has worked steadily from morning till now, except for a short rest in the shelter."

So Boaz said to Ruth,

> My daughter, listen to me. Don't go and glean in another field and don't go away from here. Stay here with my servant girls. Watch the field where the men are harvesting, and follow along after the girls. I have told the men not to touch you. And whenever you are thirsty, go and get a drink from the water jars the men have filled.
>
> Ruth 2:8–9

At this, Ruth bowed down with her face to the ground. She exclaimed, "Why have I found such favor in your eyes that you notice me—a foreigner?"

Boaz replied,

> I've been told all about what you have done for your mother-in-law since the death of your husband—how you left your father and mother and your homeland and came to live with a people you did not know before. May the Lord repay you for what you have done. May you be richly rewarded by the Lord, the God of Israel, under whose wings you have come to take refuge.
>
> Ruth 2:11–12

So Ruth worked in the field until evening. Then she threshed her barley and carried it back to Naomi, who was amazed when she saw how much Ruth had gathered. Ruth also brought Naomi her leftovers from lunch. Do you see what their relationship was like? Even while she was enjoying a meal, Ruth kept Naomi in mind.

"Where did you work? Blessed be the man who took notice of you!" Naomi was understandably impressed.

Ruth told her, "The name of the man I worked with today is Boaz."

"The Lord bless him!" Naomi said to her daughter-in-law. "[The Lord] has not stopped showing his kindness to the living and the dead." Then she added, almost as an afterthought, "That man is our close relative; he is one of our kinsman-redeemers."

God's Unexpected Blessing

See what happened? Because Ruth worked hard all day, made contact with Boaz, and brought home such a generous amount, Naomi's faith was renewed. The ministry of one faithful woman helped renew the faith of the other one who was despairing. Naomi had to admit that maybe God hadn't forgotten them after all. He certainly put Ruth in the right field.

The kinsman-redeemer was the closest male relative to a widow's late husband. And as she thought about Boaz's relationship to her family, I think the wheels in Naomi's mind suddenly started to turn. She told Ruth to stick with Boaz and not to switch to another field.

Do you notice the open communication between the two women? Naomi asked questions, Ruth answered, and there was honest dialogue between them. When we go to each other for help, or for advice, we need to tell each other everything we can think of about our circumstances. We should have open communication, with no hidden factors. Otherwise the advice and counsel we are giving may not be correct.

Of course the story of Ruth and Naomi had a happy ending. Not only did Ruth marry Boaz and provide a home for Naomi for the rest of her life, but they had a son. Generations later, a direct descendent of Ruth and Boaz was also born in Bethlehem

—His name was Jesus. How much more could God bless the friendship of two women who cared for each other so sacrificially?

I have outlined ten principles demonstrated by Naomi and Ruth which give us a model for older/younger relationships.

1. *The older woman must be a good role model.*
   Her life must attract the younger woman.

2. *The older woman must have the right motives.*
   She should not be seeking to meet her own needs, but trying to meet the needs of the younger woman.

3. *The older woman must be an encourager.*
   She should support, praise, and admonish without obligating the younger woman to herself.

4. *The older woman must be an adviser, not an authority.*
   She mustn't impose her will, but should respect the right of the younger woman to make decisions and to accept responsibility for the consequences.

5. *The relationship should be a mutual ministry.*
   The younger woman has much to offer the older woman and must contribute what she can to the relationship. It should not be a one-way street.

6. *Communication is vital.*
   There ought to be open, honest, and mutual communication at regular intervals for the relationship to flourish.

7. *Both parties have responsibilities.*
   The older is responsible to counsel, train, and protect. The younger is responsible to be teachable, to accept counsel, and to respect the wisdom of the older.

8. *God's Word must be our authority.*
   The older must instruct and advise according to God's Word and should encourage the younger to claim her blessings.

9. *Both parties can experience blessing.*

10. *Such relationships will be influential in the future.*

Investing in One Another

My life has been deeply touched by an older woman who reached out to me. I received Christ into my life when I was about seven years old. Like a lot of Christians, I was up and down spiritually. I would go to Sunday services or to a church camp and come back full of godly determination. Then, in no time, I'd be down in the valley again. Finally, when I was twenty-eight years old, married and with one little boy, I came to the end of my rope. I told the Lord that if He could not make a stable, consistent Christian out of me, I simply did not want to live any longer. Have you ever felt that way?

At the time I was attending a small, ladies' Bible class in Long Island, New York. The teacher was a slender, silver-haired woman with the most radiant smile I've ever seen. She was single and had endured a great deal of physical suffering, including a mastectomy. I'm sure that's why she was able to express God's Word with such compassion and love. Dorothy Stromberg was about fifteen years older than I, and for some reason she took an interest in me.

One day, unexpectedly, Dorothy asked me if I would be willing to teach a weekly Bible study for a handful of women. I wasn't at all sure I was the right person for the job, but agreed to try. That little class never amounted to more than about a dozen ladies, but I continued to teach it for five years. And Dorothy was always there—the class was held in her home. I know she could have taken over a hundred times and done a better job, but instead she quietly listened. She prayed. She encouraged me. I can still hear her deep, hearty chuckle. And out of her own rich spiritual insights, she shared truths with me that I have seldom learned from anyone else.

Dorothy was delighted with my children—she genuinely loved them. And she was interested in my husband and me as a couple in ways that seemed remarkable for a maiden lady nearing fifty.

As I focused my attention on God's Word and on the needs of others, my spiritual instability became less and less a problem. Meanwhile, more opportunities came along for me to teach and speak. Today, more than two decades later, the Lord has blessed me with the opportunity to speak to thousands of women every year.

Now in her seventies, Dorothy Stromberg still writes to me. That dear woman has had more influence on my life than any other person outside my family. She was there to inspire me and correct me. She loved me deeply, although we really had nothing in common except a devotion to God's Word and the desire to share it with others.

Whatever benefits you may receive from this book or from my teaching must also be credited to the account of one precious woman, Dorothy Stromberg. She invested her life in mine.

Now it's your turn! Isn't it time you invested in someone, too?

2

Women, Designed by God

*R*ev. *and Mrs. Joseph Clemmons.*

Rose smiled as she wrote the words across the top of the loan application. It always made her proud to see her name linked with Joe's. She had fallen in love with him when he was a seminary student, and it still seemed like a dream come true that they were married and that he was pastor of his own church.

Rose had been attending a college on a full-tuition scholarship when she met her future husband. She had been a high achiever in school, with a straight-A average reflecting her diligence and intelligence. Rose had always led her class, from junior high school right up to her graduation from the college.

Now, as a newlywed, she was deeply committed to Joe, their marriage, and his ministry. Joe didn't want his bride to pursue her studies or to get a job. "It really isn't appropriate for a pastor's wife, Rose."

With no papers to write, no classes to attend, and no educational goals to achieve, Rose was beginning to feel bored and restless. After weeks of inner struggle, unwilling to be disagreeable, she'd concluded, *I'll turn my energies toward making our home a place where people like to come. When people eat with us, the table will be beautiful. We'll have candles, nice china, polished silver, and linens . . .*

That morning she had decided to buy some dishes for the parsonage. Their wedding gifts had not included china, and it was evident that they would soon be entertaining a great deal. Maybe she was somewhat overenthusiastic about her new project. Nevertheless, Rose had impulsively rushed off to Macy's and was now filling out a china club application.

"Could I call my husband and ask him what his social security number is? I can't remember it . . ."

"Of course, dear." The saleswoman was more than happy to allow Rose to use the store's phone, especially if it would lead to a sale.

"Hello, Joe? I'm at Macy's buying some china, and I need to know your social security number."

"You're buying what?"

"China. For the parsonage."

Joe paused, and then quietly instructed his wife, "Don't buy anything, Rose. Come over to the office. I want to talk to you."

"Joe, there aren't any finance charges on a china club account—no interest at all. And . . ."

"No, Rose. I want to talk to you right away." Joe's voice became quite firm.

Rose was embarrassed. She politely excused herself and drove to the church. Joe's voice had sounded so hard and cold. Why?

As she sat down across the desk from her husband in his office, he solemnly opened his Bible and, in a rather business-like tone, began to read from the book of Genesis, chapter 2, verse 18.

> The Lord God said, "It is not good for the man to be alone. I will make a helper suitable for him."

"Rose," Joe spoke kindly, "God wants you to be my helper. I'll do the important stuff, and you do the detail stuff."

"What does that mean, Joe?"

"It means that if I want you to buy china, I'll tell you to buy china. I'll decide which china we should have, take care of the financing, and ask you to pick it up and put it away. Later you can fill the plates with your great cooking!" Joe winked at her.

Rose wasn't especially flattered by Joe's compliment. Surely he expected her to be more than a cook. "But I'm perfectly capable of making decisions myself."

"That's not the way God planned it, Rose. You are my helper, remember? You know women really aren't emotionally equipped to make important decisions. And besides," he smiled proudly, "that's what I'm here for!"

What Are We Supposed to Think?

Like many men, including some seminary graduates, Joe hasn't learned everything there is to know about God's Word. Or about marriage. Or about women.

Recent decades have placed a woman's role, her rights, and her responsibilities center stage in the arena of world opinion. There has been statement and counter-statement, action and reaction. And there has been change. Some changes have had negative implications when weighed against Christian values. Others have been positive and productive.

Our culture's focus on women has forced the church to rethink its position. What is biblical and what is traditional? And are they one and the same? Or has tradition gone beyond what the Bible really says? Books on the subject abound, and it is mind-boggling to try and determine whose perspective is the right one.

What are we supposed to believe? We can't judge truth without a standard for truth. If we are believers in Jesus Christ, His inspired Scripture has to serve as that standard for us.

The next few pages contain some of the most basic, foundational lessons in this book. Once you understand God's original design for women, I hope you will be able to eliminate wrong concepts and faulty ideas from your mind. Like the young pastor in our story, you and the women to whom you minister may have been living under some serious misconceptions for a lifetime.

In the Image of the Creator

Just what did God have in mind for us when He created woman? Was she an afterthought? Or was she the final word of completion in His beautiful, perfect world? As always, the best place to start is at the very beginning.

> Then God said, "Let us make man in our image, in our likeness, and let them rule over the fish of the sea and the birds of the air, over the livestock, over all the earth, and over all the creatures that move along the ground."
> So God created man in his own image, in the image of God he created him; male and female he created them. God blessed them and said to them, "Be fruitful and increase in number; fill the earth and subdue it. Rule over the fish of the sea and the birds of the air and over every living creature that moves on the ground." . . .
> God saw all that he had made, and it was very good.
>
> Genesis 1:26–28, 31

The most distinctive thing about our human race is that it is created in God's image. That is the line of demarcation between us and the rest of Creation. We are like Him but not identical to Him. "Image" implies that we are to mirror God. That is why we were created in the first place.

By the way, please don't make the mistake of thinking that "man" being made in God's image refers to males only. Man is the generic name for the human race, while male and female refer to sexual differentiations. Man is the image of God, woman is the image of God, and together they give the complete image of God because there are both male and female aspects to the character of God. Man and woman are different but equal. Do you notice any superiority or inferiority implied with regard to either one in the Genesis account? No, there is none.

What does "in the image of God" mean? God is not a force and not a thing; He is a person. And both the male and the female are persons, too.

People Who Need People

I'm grateful to Dr. Larry Crabb for some of the following insights.

Because we are persons, God has built within us a rightful hunger for relationship, a longing for impact. Those needs for relationship and impact are built-in and legitimate. It's only when we try to meet them ourselves, without depending on God, that we get into trouble.

A young woman may come to you and say, "I just want to be married, and that's all I really need to be happy." God created her with that longing for a lasting relationship. After all, we were created in God's image and the Godhead is relational. God is a triune being—Father, Son, and Holy Spirit. Don't rebuke her for her desire. Just encourage her to wait for God's choice and God's time.

Spirit, Mind, Heart, and Will

What are some of the components of being a person? Besides being relational, male and female human beings have an equivalent spiritual capacity—we are spirit beings. This distinguishes us from animals, because as spirit beings we have the ability to know God. When we are born, we don't know God without being introduced to Him, but the capacity to know Him is inherently there. Adam and Eve knew God—they walked and talked with Him.

In addition to being spiritual, we are created as rational beings, with the ability to think and reason. When Adam and

Eve were created they had an extra benefit intellectually—their minds were not yet darkened by sin.

Whether male or female, we are also emotional beings. Emotions are perfectly appropriate and are part of our created nature.

Furthermore, we are volitional. That means we are able to choose, to decide. We aren't robots, preprogrammed to certain actions. As a matter of fact, if Adam and Eve had been so controlled, the "fall of man" would probably never have happened.

Acting Out a God-given Destiny

Both Adam and Eve were persons, made in the image of God. And, as persons, they had several functions—things they were to do. They were equals in both their responsibility and accountability. God blessed both Adam and Eve, and as one of their functions, He gave them dominion over the earth as coregents.

Another of their primary functions was to "be fruitful and increase in number," obviously referring to reproduction. Now we know for certain that this was said to both male and female, because neither could do it alone. Adam and Eve were equal partners in reproducing their own kind. This tells us something very important about our sexuality. Sexual relationship existed in marriage before the Fall. Sex is good and pure and part of God's gracious provision for mankind.

Adam and Eve were also expected to function by living in obedience to their Maker.

> And the Lord God commanded the man, "You are free to eat from any tree in the garden; but you must not eat from the tree of the knowledge of good and evil, for when you eat of it you will surely die."
>
> Genesis 2:16–17

Adam and Eve were jointly responsible to obey God. He said, "You can eat of all the trees in the garden. There's just one you cannot eat of." Why do you think God put this one prohibition in place? I believe His purpose was to test their will. When these two were created they were of the highest possible intelligence. But unless we acknowledge God as our authority, it's easy to become proud and independent.

A Design of Immense Value

Woman was created to share equal value with man. The single woman and the married woman alike are complete in their relationship to God through Christ. Our value does not come from being attached to or accepted by a man. Nor does our value decrease because a man has rejected us. If we understand that, we will have a much healthier view of men, marriage relationships, and what to expect from our husbands.

Just remember this: Women are of equal value to men; equal in personhood, and equal in responsibility. And our immense value lies in the fact that we are made in the image of God.

It is interesting to note that before sin entered the picture, there was no need to emphasize the headship of the husband. Eve was a co-ruler, not one of those ruled.

Never Meant to Be Alone

Man and woman were created to be equal. But they were also created to be different.

> The Lord God formed man from the dust of the ground and breathed into his nostrils the breath of life, and the man became a living being. . . . The Lord God said, "It is not good for the man to be alone, I will make a helper suitable for him."
>
> Genesis 2:7, 18

Man's aloneness was the first thing in Creation that was not good. It was never intended that he be isolated and alone. His personhood was affected because human beings are made for relationships. His function was affected because he could not reproduce, could not do all he was intended to do without someone to complete him—someone who was like him.

The full expression of humanity required the creation of the woman.

The Genesis text continues:

> Now the Lord God had formed out of the ground all the beasts of the field and all the birds of the air. He brought them to the man to see what he would name them; and whatever the man called each living creature, that was its name. So the man gave names to all the livestock, the birds of the air and all the beasts of the field.
>
> But for Adam no suitable helper was found.
>
> Genesis 2:19–20

God gave Adam the responsibility for naming all the animals He had created. Why did God make Adam go through this procedure before He gave him his own mate? I believe He wanted him to realize that he had a need. Surely the implication here is that all the animals came before him, and each one had a counterpart that resembled it. Lion and lioness. He-wolf and she-wolf. Goose and gander.

Can you picture Adam? He was gazing across that vast host of animals passing before him, looking all the way down to the end of the line, hoping to find somebody like himself. But for Adam no corresponding person could be found—no one like himself.

God wanted him to recognize his uniqueness and his incompleteness. Most of all, he wanted Adam to be aware that he had no ability to meet his own needs.

Doesn't God do that with you and me? He gets us into situations where we're helpless, where we feel like we have no place to turn. Finally we say, "Okay, God! I don't know what I am going to do. I guess I'll just have to depend on you to provide for me."

Then He says, "That's the idea! That's why I brought you into such an impossible situation in the first place. Now I'll give you what you need."

Much More Than a Helper

And so it was that the first "surgery" was performed, along with the first anesthesia.

> So the Lord God caused the man to fall into a deep sleep; and while he was sleeping, he took one of the man's ribs and closed up the place with flesh. Then the Lord God made a woman from the rib he had taken out of the man, and he brought her to the man.
>   The man said,
>
>> "This is now bone of my bones
>>   and flesh of my flesh;
>> she shall be called 'woman,'
>>   for she was taken out of man."
>
>   Genesis 2:21–23

God said something significant about the woman He made. He said she was to be a "suitable helper," two words which are translated in the King James Bible as "helpmeet." Most women react to that word with annoyance. "That makes me mad!" they complain. "A helpmeet is nothing but a doormat!"

Well, "doormat" is not the meaning of the biblical word—not at all. "Helper" is the word *ezer*, a term used about nineteen times in the Old Testament. Four times it is used to describe a man helping another man, indicating that a peer was assisting a peer. However, on no fewer than fifteen other occasions it refers to God helping man. God is our Helper—our *Ezer*.

Clearly, God is a superior being helping an inferior one. "Helper" is never used of an inferior helping a superior.

We usually think of the helper as the dummy who hands over the tools to the smart guy. But this word helper expresses something far different. Helper means that woman's nature, her disposition, and her abilities supply what is lacking in man, and vice versa. They had to be different but equal to complete each other.

In short, a helper is one who assists another in reaching complete fulfillment. There is nothing demeaning about that, is there?

Marriage Made in Heaven

It was God who brought Eve to Adam. In this first marriage we learn a lot about God's standard for our own marriages. First, marriage is God's institution and it represents His absolute best for man and woman. Don't forget, before they disobeyed God, those two people were intended to live forever. If sin had not entered the scene, neither one would have died. Every human would have had one mate forever. You can see how serious God was about marriage when He originally initiated it.

"For this reason a man will leave his father and mother and be united to his wife and they will become one flesh" (Gen. 2:24). The marriage relationship is supposed to take priority over every other human relationship, including the tight bond between parent and child.

The man is to leave home and become the head of a new family. Each man was to take his wife away from both his family and hers in order to form a separate unit. This doesn't mean that they were to desert their parents, as though they no longer cared for them. It does mean that they left behind their parents' authority, along with their dependence upon Mom and Dad. If we really took this idea to heart, it would eliminate a great many in-law problems.

The marriage relationship was to be permanent. The word "cleave," which is translated "united" in the New International Version, is the word for glue. The husband was to be permanently glued to his wife. It meant that this was an indissoluble union and that man and woman were to be united in a one-flesh process. The Bible doesn't say that they were to be one flesh, it says that they were to become one flesh. That process continues for a lifetime.

Let's consider for a moment the definition of the word flesh. Flesh is not just talking about the body. To become one flesh means becoming a spiritual, moral, intellectual, and physical unity. The sexual union, which is the distinctive of marriage, should symbolize the uniting of two personalities in the lifelong process of becoming one flesh.

Do you see why sexual immorality is such a desecration of what God originally intended? Sexual intercourse represents a uniting of two personalities. It is not supposed to satisfy some irresistible, sensual appetite that can be fed from any source available.

In Genesis 2:25 we read, "The man and his wife were both naked, and they felt no shame." Here is true intimacy. Intimacy means that the basic heart needs of a human being are being consistently understood and met. You and I, because we are fallen people, cannot even begin to understand what this involves.

But Adam and Eve were naked without shame. Their relationship was one of complete openness. They were thoroughly vulnerable and trusting. They had no hidden motives. They felt no fear of exploitation. Their love was unhindered by criticism or rejection, and it flowed freely between them.

I know what you're thinking—"I can't even imagine what that would be like." But that is exactly the way it was in the beginning. There was nothing unpleasant between Adam and Eve to hinder their intimacy. Tragically, that sublime intimacy was the very first thing affected by their sin. We'll look at that more closely in the next chapter.

All Women Are Created Equal

As we meditate upon Creation, God's original intention for woman emerges more clearly in our minds. It's exceptionally important for us to understand who we really are intended to be. Before we are able to reach out to other women we must have a proper perspective on our own value as persons. We must also grasp our responsibility to function as God intended. Then we will be able to share it with other women.

Dr. Allen Ross of Dallas Theological Seminary has written an excellent position paper on women. I'd like to quote his summary comment:

> She (woman) is his (man's) peer, his equal in capacities of intellect, moral worth and sensibility. She can think, feel, imagine, reason. She can sell goods, plan buildings, make statues, diagnose diseases, construct philosophies or write epics. In a word, what is open to a man as a human being is open to her.

Men and women are the special handiwork of God, they both have the same nature and they both have a spiritual and moral capacity from God.

A Place of Her Own

Charlotte is a refined, well-manicured redhead with a marvelous sense of humor. Women love her down-to-earth style and her practical approach to Christianity. She grew up in a home where the Word of God was respected and treasured, and she has carried that reverence for Scripture into her adult life.

For years her pastor asked her to lead a women's Bible class, and for years she refused. But deep inside, Charlotte knew she was gifted, and she longed to share with other women her love for God, His ways, and His message.

But she hadn't shared her longing with her husband, Richard. A highly successful land developer, he had banked his first million before he was thirty years old. And his favorite pastime was making spontaneous trips here, there, and everywhere.

Richard might arrive home on Friday night with two first-class tickets to Hawaii. Or he might call on Wednesday,

"Charlotte, can you meet me at the airport tonight? I want to go to London for the rest of the week." She had long ago learned to keep a current passport in her always-packed overnight bag. On more than one occasion she had actually been on her way overseas in less than an hour's time.

Charlotte's friends envied her. How could anyone complain about an arrangement like that? Richard was a man who loved living, and nothing made him happier than sharing life with his beautiful wife. But, in an odd way, Charlotte was trapped by his spontaneity. She couldn't make long-range plans. In fact, she couldn't commit herself to anything more than a few days in the future.

Charlotte and I had a talk about her unique problem. "I feel guilty complaining, Vickie. I know Richard is one in a million . . ."

"Well, I have to admit, I've certainly heard worse problems."

Charlotte laughed. "I know, I know. The most important thing is, I don't want to hurt Richard. I hate to even bring it up. But, you know, it's more than just wanting to teach, Vickie."

"What do you mean?"

"I mean my whole identity is wrapped up in being Richard's wife. I want something of my own—something to give me satisfaction without depending on his money or his success. Does that sound terrible? I'm sorry if it does."

"No, in fact I think those are healthy feelings. God gave you gifts that Richard doesn't have, and you should be using them. As a matter of fact, he should be helping you use them!"

"I sure don't want to hurt him . . ." It appeared to me that Charlotte and Richard were genuinely devoted to each other.

"You don't need to hurt him at all. Explain to him that you feel God has given you a special gift of teaching, and that you'd really like to be using it. But you don't want to miss any opportunities to travel with him, either. Ask him if he could possibly give you a schedule for the next few months so you can make arrangements both to teach and to travel."

"Don't you think he'll be offended?"

"Why should he? It's his responsibility to help you become everything God intended you to be. And it's obvious to everyone who knows you, God intended for you to teach His Word."

Charlotte made up her mind to try. And fortunately, Richard really is one in a million. A committed Christian himself, he was wonderfully cooperative when his wife brought up the subject of teaching. He agreed that she should give it a try, and he immediately scheduled their trips around the Wednesday-night commitment she wanted to make.

The experiment worked better than either of them had dared hope. Today, Charlotte sets aside about one-third of the year for teaching, and her classes are packed with women. The rest of the year she is free to come and go with Richard, wherever his wanderlust may carry them.

"I'm proud of her," he told me one day. "She's got so much to offer, it wouldn't be right for me to keep her all to myself!"

Two of a Kind

The facts are irrefutable, both in biblical teaching and in practical experience. Male and female together were created equally in God's image. They were meant to be in perfect harmony with each other and with their Creator. They were to function as His representatives on earth, equally blessed, equally ruling, equally reproducing, and equally responsible to worship God in obedience.

We must reject, authoritatively on the basis of God's word, manmade notions about a "woman's place" (usually in the kitchen!). We must not accept ideas about her inferiority either intellectually, emotionally, morally, or spiritually. We were created to complete mankind in God's image. We are intended to act as godly counterparts to males, because our natures supply what is lacking in theirs. Most of all, we were declared, by our Creator, to be "very good."

As women, God is for us. Who can be against us?

3

What Went Wrong?

Susan smiled as she brushed a damp strand of hair behind her ear and sank wearily into a chair. She had completely rearranged the living room furniture and had bought some new accent pillows and plants. The task completed, she was delighted with the results.

It looks like a different house! she thought to herself as she proudly surveyed the results. *I just hope Jack likes it . . . he'll be home any minute.* At the thought of Jack's possible reaction, fear rippled inside her. *It just depends on his mood . . .* The sound of the front door latch interrupted her thoughts.

"What on earth?" Susan's husband Jack stood in the doorway with a deep scowl on his face. "What do you think you're doing?"

Susan was immediately apologetic. "I'm sorry Jack . . . I wanted to surprise you. I thought a change would be good . . ." Her voice was a little shaky, and her words faded into silence.

Jack looked at her coldly. "You know better than that. Haven't we been through this before? I'm the head of this house, and you are supposed to ask my permission before you make any decisions!"

Summoning her courage, Susan murmured, "But it's my house, too, Jack!"

"Look, Susan. This is a *Christian* home, and I'm the head of the house. You can check your Bible if you want. But you're rebelling against God's plan for marriage when you don't ask me before you make decisions."

"My other Christian friends have more freedom than I do." By now Susan was almost pleading. Enraged, Jack took several steps over to her, grabbed her upper arms and shook her firmly.

"Look, Susan, you're a *woman*. The Bible says that your husband is supposed to rule over you!" He abruptly released her from his grasp, and she fell back into the chair, trembling and terrified.

Jack folded his arms and glared down at her. "I want this furniture put back the way it was, and I want everything you bought returned to the store. Maybe you've learned a lesson and maybe you haven't, Susan. But I'm the head of the house and you're going to obey me. Whether you like it or not, that's the way it's supposed to be!"

The Devil's Plan

God created a wonderful world—beautiful, harmonious, and perfect. And he designed relationships between men and women to be completely fulfilling and satisfying. But when we look around, instead of friendship we see misunderstanding and resentment. Instead of cooperation, we see conflict. Instead of compassion, we see abuse—both physical and emotional. Why isn't the world the way God wanted it to be? What went wrong?

In the third chapter of Genesis we encounter a sinister being whose actions and intentions dramatically disagree with those of the Creator God. Satan's first appearance in Scripture is most instructive for us. You have to remember that although Satan is much more intelligent than we are, he is not omniscient, omnipresent, or omnipotent. However, he has had a long time to polish his strategies. And, believe me, what he did in the Garden of Eden he is still doing today. In fact, he's not even original—he keeps repeating the same deceits he's always practiced.

Now the serpent was more crafty than any of the wild animals the Lord God had made. He said to the woman, "Did God really say, 'You must not eat from any tree in the garden'?"

The woman said to the serpent, "We may eat fruit from the trees in the garden, but God did say, 'You must not eat fruit from the tree that is in the middle of the garden, and you must not touch it, or you will die.'"

"You will not surely die," the serpent said to the woman. "For God knows that when you eat of it your eyes will be opened, and you will be like God, knowing good and evil."

When the woman saw that the fruit of the tree was good for food and pleasing to the eye, and also desirable for gaining wisdom, she took some and ate it. She also gave some to her husband, who was with her, and he ate it. Then the eyes of both of them were opened, and they realized they were naked; so they sewed fig leaves together and made coverings for themselves.

Genesis 3:1–7

Masks and Masquerades

From the beginning, Satan's entire purpose has been to deceive and destroy. That was his intention then, and it's his intention now. It didn't matter whether he approached Adam or Eve—either one would do because they were one flesh and they were joint rulers of the earth. Sometimes we hear statements like, "He came to the woman because he knew she was weaker. She was more emotional and a little less balanced." I don't believe that's the case at all. I think Satan approached Eve because she was so influential with her husband.

The first thing we notice is that Satan appeared in disguise. The serpent was an animal, and one with high intelligence. He is described as "crafty," which means he was clever and smart. It was through the body and the mouth of this animal that Satan spoke.

Satan usually comes to us incognito, and it's no wonder. If we saw him as the Prince of Darkness we wouldn't want anything to do with him. So he comes to us in various forms, and often as an angel of light. "I come to you with knowledge; I come to you with enlightenment. What I have to offer is really good for you." That's what he says, and that's why people fall for it.

How subtly Satan posed his question: "Did God really say you must not eat from any tree in the garden?" He emphasized God's prohibition and not His lavish provision. Isn't that the way we often view life? We look at the flaws instead of all the good things about our circumstances, our husbands, our children, our parents.

I think it's important for us to observe that Eve was not yet created when God gave the rules about the tree of the knowledge of good and evil to Adam. What she knew she had heard second-hand. So she explained to Satan that they couldn't eat from the tree or even touch it, because they would die if they did.

Satan immediately retorted, "You will not surely die."

An Evil Pair of Lies

There are two basic tactics that Satan still uses against men and women. The first is to make us doubt God's Word. In this case, he boldly declared that nothing would happen if Adam and Eve disobeyed God. He contradicted the spoken word of God, and asserted that they could defy His rules without consequences.

Satan's second tactic was to tempt Eve to distrust God's character. What Satan implied was, "God doesn't really love you, and He isn't doing what is best for you. He's keeping something from you that you really ought to have. And He's doing it with dishonorable motives—He doesn't want you to be like Him." What foolishness! Adam and Eve were already like Him. They were made in His image.

Jesus says in John 8:44, "he [Satan] is a liar and the father of lies." And his two big lies are right here: God's Word is not true, and God is not good.

I think that most of our spiritual problems come from these two basic untruths. We don't believe His Word, so we disobey what He's told us. We doubt His goodness and question His love for us, so we try to take care of ourselves in our own way. Sometimes we feel that if we say, "God, I just want Your will," He's sure to bring the worst thing in the world upon us. We assume God imposes His sovereignty on us by forcing us to do what we most hate. We don't really believe He is a good God.

As for Eve, what was her response? Notice that her attention was now focused on the forbidden tree.

> When the woman saw that the fruit of the tree was good for food and pleasing to the eye, and also desirable for gaining wisdom, she took some and ate it. She also gave some to her husband, who was with her, and he ate it.
>
> Genesis 3:6

Satan plays a successful game, and he has an impressive record of wins. We see his three best weapons in 1 John 2:16: "The lust of the flesh, the lust of the eyes and the pride of life" (KJV). Satan always approaches us through these same channels.

Satan's purpose was to cause Adam and Eve to act independently of God. "Listen," he warned them, "God is not taking care of you the way He should. You have to take care of yourselves!"

One of today's psychological gurus, Abraham Maslow, says, "Fulfillment and growth come from close attention to the needs of the Self." Self becomes sovereign instead of the true God. That is exactly what Eve chose to do—she looked at the tree and its fruit and said, "That's good! I should eat it." She discarded revelation from God and replaced it with human reasoning. She chose instant pleasure over obedience to God's instruction. "I really need to become wise," she said.

How often does our own intelligence stand between us and simple, childlike faith?

Deceived or Disobedient?

Eve saw the fruit, concluded that she needed it, and then gave it to her husband *who was with her.* I wonder why Adam didn't interrupt the process. He was with her! Why didn't he say, "No, we shouldn't do this"? The Scripture is careful not to put the blame on Eve. It says, instead, that she was thoroughly deceived (1 Tim. 2:14). More responsibility was placed on Adam, who completely understood what he was doing.

In Romans 5:12 and 17, we read that *through one man sin entered into the world.* Adam is given responsibility for the fall. This tells me something—that we women have a great influence, so great that it must always be godly. Adam had to choose whether to follow a fallen mate or to obey God. He chose Eve.

You will notice how God deals with the two of them.

> Then the man and his wife heard the sound of the Lord God as he was walking in the garden in the cool of the day, and they hid from the Lord God among the trees of the garden. But the Lord God called to the man, "Where are you?"
>
> He answered, "I heard you in the garden, and I was afraid because I was naked; so I hid."
>
> And he said, "Who told you that you were naked? Have you eaten from the tree that I commanded you not to eat from?"
>
> The man said, "The woman you put here with me, she gave me some fruit from the tree and I ate it."
>
> Then the Lord God said to the woman, "What is this you have done?"
>
> The woman said, "The serpent deceived me, and I ate."
>
> Genesis 3:8–13

Lost Innocence, Lost Intimacy

The first evident consequence of Adam and Eve's disobedience was its toll on their marital relationship. They noticed that they were naked and they covered themselves with fig leaves. From whom were they hiding themselves? From each other. There was nobody else there. Immediately, guilt and shame entered into their open, vulnerable love. The intimacy of the marriage was gravely damaged. There was no longer complete trust. Instead there was fear of exploitation and, with it, insecurity. And, of course, there was blame.

Karen sat down across from Phil as he read the newspaper. She put her hand on his arm, gently stroking it. *I hate to interrupt him*, she thought, *but we've got to communicate*.

She spoke softly. "How was your day, Honey?"

He paused a moment, making quite an effort to lift his eyes from the sports page. "Fine." He smiled, nodded, and resumed his reading.

"Anything exciting happen?"

Again, a pause. And this time, when Phil answered there was an ever-so-slight edge to his voice. "Nope. Nothing exciting." He smiled politely again, turned a page, and continued to read.

"Honey, I need to talk to you about something I've been thinking about. Something is really troubling me, and I need you to help me understand."

"Hmmmm?" Phil didn't look up, and Karen wasn't sure if he was listening.

"I need to talk to you." When she repeated the words a little more loudly, Phil folded the paper and laid it down. He sighed in resignation, crossed his arms, and said, "Okay, so what's the problem?"

"Oh, it's not really a problem, Phil. It's just that I've been feeling a little bad about myself, and I wanted to talk to you about it."

"There's nothing wrong with you. You're fine."

"But I'm just not myself at the moment. I don't look as good as I used to, and . . .

"You look fine to me, Baby." Phil raised his eyebrows and smiled flirtatiously. "In fact, I think you look terrific. You want to go talk about it in the bedroom?"

Tears stung Karen's eyes. *Why is it always like this?* she asked herself. "No, that's not what I mean, Phil. Can't we talk about it here? I'm just kind of depressed, and . . ."

"I know what you need." He reached for her, and she pulled away instinctively.

"That's *not* what I need!"

"Oh, Honey, of course it is. You just need a little lovin', that's all."

"Phil," Karen snapped at him. "It's your fault we can't communicate with each other. I hope you realize that."

Insulted, Phil picked up the paper again. "Hey, look. If you want to buy some new clothes or something, just go ahead. Anyway, you're the one with the problem. Not me. I'm perfectly happy with you."

Karen jumped up, her face flushed with anger and frustration. "What I need is for you to listen to me for once instead of always trying to get me into bed. All you're interested in is satisfying your stupid sex drive. You couldn't care less about who I am or what I want!" With that, she stormed out of the room.

Phil stared sadly at the doorway for a moment. "Women!" he muttered. "I'll never understand them. Aren't they ever happy?"

The loss of intimacy between men and women first occurred in the Garden of Eden. And it continues today, along with its accompanying maladies—mistrust, misunderstanding, and manipulation.

When God confronted Adam with his disobedience, Adam's answer was to blame his wife, then to blame God because He put Eve there with him.

Our sinful nature drives us to protect ourselves. We blame others in order to shed responsibility from ourselves. The first step toward getting ourselves straightened out is to admit our responsibility and to humbly take the consequences for our own actions.

Someday you may counsel with a woman who shares with you the fact that she has committed a terrible sin. Perhaps she's beginning to feel the consequences of it. Explain how she can find forgiveness through the Lord Jesus Christ and encourage her to accept God's forgiveness. Then you'll want to help her understand that while the consequences are always part of the package, God is still there to give us strength to bear them.

If you can encourage her to admit that she's responsible for her wrongdoing, she'll be able to move forward, taking some essential steps toward recovery.

Learning to Be Afraid

The first relationship visibly affected by sin was the one between husband and wife. But Adam and Eve's relationship with God was also broken. He came to them. He initiated contact. He made the move for reconciliation. He said to Adam, "Where are you?" Of course, He already knew.

Adam said, "I was afraid, so I hid."

Fear is the first emotion named in the Bible. It came as a result of sin. What was Adam afraid of? Punishment? Exposure? He and Eve first hid from each other; then they hid from God. In both cases they acted to protect themselves. God had said, "For when you eat of it you will surely die." We know that Adam did not physically die until he was 930 years old. So wonderful was the first created body that it took nine centuries for it to expire. The physical consequences of disobedience didn't happen immediately.

But something else did. Spiritual death transpires when man's spirit is separated from God. And that is what happened instantly. We know it happened because instead of walking with God in love and in communion, Adam and Eve were afraid and hid from Him. Spiritual death occurred, even though Satan said it wouldn't happen.

Curses and More Curses

God's next move was to give Adam, Eve, and Satan a preview of coming attractions. He told them, "This is the way the world is going to work as a result of your sin." Then He cursed Satan, who spoke through the serpent.

> And I will put enmity between you and the woman, and between your offspring and hers; he will crush your head, and you will strike his heel.

> Genesis 3:15

There is something wonderful here. At the same time that sin and its consequences fell upon the whole world, God gave the first promise of the Savior. He said to the serpent, "I will put enmity between you and the woman and between your seed and hers" (KJV).

"Seed" always refers to a man's offspring in the Scriptures. This is the only place where it refers to a woman's seed. Of course it is looking ahead to the virgin birth, where Christ is born of a woman without a man's involvement. Right here at the dawn of creation, just as sin appeared, God was promising to send a Savior. The promise was made to Satan. The promise was kept through a woman.

Pain, Longing, and Humiliation

When God spoke to the woman with regard to her consequences, he didn't say "because." God knew that she had been deceived. But He did say,

> I will greatly increase your pains in childbearing; with pain you will give birth to children. Your desire will be for your husband, and he will rule over you.

> Genesis 3:16

For woman, what was meant to be pleasurable became painful. There would be misery both in childbearing and child rearing. Eve experienced this poignantly when her second child was murdered by her first.

The expression, "Your desire will be for your husband" has had many interpretations. I think it predicts a wife's yearning for intimacy that is not reciprocated by her husband. I believe every woman, at one time or another, has felt this longing for intimacy with her mate—a longing that he just would not or could not meet. Someone has put it this way, "Woman wants a mate but she gets a master. She wants a lover but she gets a lord."

For Eve, the first result of sin was distress in mothering. The second was domination, a complete mastery by the man. This was never God's original intention, and it most certainly was never His command. "And he will rule over you" was, however, a prediction—and how true it has been throughout history.

Instead of being one of the two original rulers, woman is now one of the ones ruled. Since God first spoke those prophetic words, the heartless domination and exploitation of women has occurred worldwide. This is especially true in non-Christian cultures where women are often viewed as nothing more than property.

History speaks for itself: Jesus Christ is the only true liberator of women. Unfortunately, even where Christ is known, I do not believe that the full extent of the scriptural liberation of women has been clarified. The domination of man over woman is an ongoing reality within many of our churches, despite the fact that it is certainly not taught in Ephesians 5. There the husband lovingly lays down his life for his wife, sacrificially and in selfless love. In response to his devotion and commitment, she voluntarily submits to him.

Blood, Sweat, and Tears

As God continued to spell out the aftermath of the sinful episode in Eden, the man was affected both in his person and in his function. God said,

"Because you listened to your wife and ate from the tree about which I commanded you, 'You must not eat of it,' cursed is the ground because of you; through painful toil you will eat of it all the days of your life. It will produce thorns and thistles for you, and you will eat the plants of the field. By the sweat of your brow you will eat your food until you return to the ground, since from it you were taken; for dust you are and to dust you will return."

Genesis 3:17–19

The death sentence fell upon Adam. Furthermore, he was thrown out of the garden into a world where the soil resisted cultivation, where thorns and thistles grew, where he would experience a lifetime of struggle and toil. Now there would be physical death as well as spiritual. Instead of perfect fellowship there would be alienation and conflict.

But here, in the midst of sin and death, God made wonderful provision for His fallen creatures.

The Lord God made garments of skin for Adam and his wife and clothed them. And the Lord God said, "The man has now become like one of us, knowing good and evil. He must not be allowed to reach out his hand and take also from the tree of life and eat, and live forever." So the Lord God banished him from the Garden of Eden to work the ground from which he had been taken.

Genesis 3:21–23

A Portrait of Redemption

In all their shame, Adam and Eve had covered themselves with fig leaves. But God covered them with skins. And in doing so, He taught them a glorious lesson. He had already alluded to a Savior. Now He gave them a picture of what the Savior would do.

God killed two lambs and made coverings for Adam and Eve from their skins. And what did the man and woman learn?

For one thing, they witnessed the fact that sin caused death, and that without the shedding of blood there is no forgiveness. They also learned that God was the only one who could provide a substitute suitable to take their penalty. What a superb picture of Jesus!

Sin entered the picture, and Paradise was shattered. God's exquisite creation was perverted by evil. And that evil is still with us today.

So—what has changed and what remains the same?

Humankind—Scarred and Crippled by Sin

Are we still created in God's image? Yes, although the image is marred and flawed.

Are we still persons? Yes, and as persons we still have a thirst for relationship and for impact. But now those needs often go unmet, and we are inclined to use wrong strategies to satisfy them.

Self-protection has now become our major goal. Why? Because at the core of every one of us is fear. Down deep inside me is the fear that if you really knew me you would not like me. So I put on a superficial layer of something I hope gives me acceptability. You are the same, and you have a layer of acceptability, too. When we meet, we bump into each other's layers, but we seldom really get to know one another. Fear of exposure, fear of wrong motives, fear of exploitation, fear of rejection—these keep us from being real with each other.

Are we still rational beings? Yes, but now our minds are darkened and we quickly believe a lie. We can reason, but we can't really know how the universe fits together. We don't know how to make our world work without a knowledge of God. That is why human philosophy is so irrelevant. When there is no acknowledgment of God, society's "great minds" substitute all kinds of logical-sounding concepts. But there is nothing of substance, only empty jargon and disappointing results. Apart from God there is no truth.

We are still emotional beings, but now our emotions can be destructive, leading us away from God instead of toward Him. We are still volitional beings, but now we choose unrighteousness. Even righteous things are sometimes done for the wrong reasons.

We are still in dominion over the earth, but now we exploit the earth to satisfy our greed. Meanwhile, we live in a hostile world rather than the perfect environment of Eden's garden.

Marriage—A House Divided

But of all the consequences sin brought upon humanity, the wonderful relationship of marriage has been the most tragically affected. Instead of intimacy, there is intimidation. Instead of equals, man and woman have become enemies. Instead of completing one another, there is now competition. And instead of having dominion, woman is now dominated.

Sexuality remains an integral part of our lives. Sex was originally intended for unity and oneness, for parenthood, for pleasure and for the prevention of immorality (1 Corinthians 7). Now it has become an appetite. Like hunger or thirst, it is viewed as something that must be satisfied at any cost. Sex has been removed from the protection of marriage, and the results are self-evident. Multiple partners. Serial marriages. Group sex. Homosexuality. Abortion. Venereal diseases. AIDS.

Reclaiming God's Perfect Plan

It was mankind's disobedience that brought the curse and its devastation upon Paradise. But Christ came to redeem us from that curse. If you have not trusted Jesus Christ as your Savior, there is no hope of reconciliation between God and you. There are no fig leaves that God will accept—no membership in the church, no good works, no being a nice wife and a good mother—none of this will do. You must recognize that you are a sinner by nature. That the punishment for sin is death. That Jesus Christ died in your place on the cross. That He rose from the dead. That He is the only substitute God will accept.

What is redemption? Redemption means that God has bought you back for Himself through the blood of His Son. It means that He has made a way for you to walk with Him and talk with Him, just as Adam and Eve once did. It means that sin no longer separates you from Him.

Once you have received God's redemption, some profound changes will occur. Some of the effects of the curse will be removed from your life! When we trust Christ, salvation changes the way we live. It also transforms the way we view life. We can go back to Genesis 1 and 2 in order to understand what God had in mind for us in the first place. And then we can begin, by faith, to live that way—right now.

Christ's redemptive power at work in us will enable us to reclaim our proper role as women—the women God intended us to be. Our integrity as persons can be restored. Our functions can be realigned with His will. And our God-given authority can be reinstated.

His redemption should put us on guard to protect our marriages. Once we realize how much God believes in marriage and how much Satan is against it, we will be on the alert. In the Garden of Eden, Satan didn't attack the man until he was married. I believe Satan's purpose today is to break up Christian homes, and he is having a heyday. We should unite with our husbands against the real enemy.

Through redemption, those who are single and redeemed can be brought to perfect completion in Christ. Whether His ultimate will for us is marriage or not, He has promised to complete the good work He has begun in us through Christ Jesus our Lord.

Are you redeemed? Yes, you are if you have trusted Jesus Christ as your Lord and Savior. Once you've received God's redemption, you can be restored, to some degree, to His original design for you. God's Spirit will transform your mind. He will bring health to your emotions. He will redirect your will. He will breathe new life into your spirit. He will define and develop your own special role as a woman.

Redemption means that you can stop believing the lies of the enemy.

Redemption assures you that God is a good God.

Redemption frees you from the powerful control of sin.

Redemption establishes your value before a Holy God.

Redemption proves that God loves you and that God's Word really does come true.

4

Making Love, Sharing Love

*W*hen I first spoke to Christa I was impressed by her delicate beauty. She was a slender blonde with pale, Scandinavian blue eyes.

"Vickie," she looked directly in my eyes as she spoke, a deep frown creasing her brow, "I have a big problem with sex, and I don't know how to solve it."

"What kind of problem, Christa?"

"Well, Kevin and I have been married for five years. We had a wild affair before that. In fact, to be honest, I took him away from his first wife." She shook her head and looked down at her hands. "I'm not proud of that, you know."

I waited for her to continue, and after a few seconds she went on.

"When Kevin and I were seeing each other, we had the most exciting sex life imaginable. It was just amazing. I got excited just thinking about him when he was away. And the minute we were face to face, we couldn't keep our hands off each other. Frankly, I loved every minute of it, even though it was wrong."

"So you're married now. What's happened?"

She looked at me with the most puzzled expression on her face, searching for words. Suddenly her voice broke, tears flooded her face, and she whispered hoarsely, "I can't stand for him to touch me!"

"What happens when he touches you?"

"I feel filthy—like a whore! I'm so sorry for the things we did. I really am. We broke his first wife's heart, and it was all because of sex. Sure we have a good relationship otherwise, but that's what caused all the trouble. I hate sex!"

"Have you asked God to forgive you for your past sins?"

Christa's voice was muffled. "Yes . . . but I can't forgive myself."

"And have you forgiven Kevin?"

"Kevin? You mean for dragging me into it in the first place?" An unexpected tone of bitterness tinged her voice. She studied me thoughtfully before she answered. "No, I guess I haven't. In fact I've never even thought about it."

"Christa, you are going to have to forgive yourself. If God has already forgiven you, how can you refuse to forgive yourself? And as for Kevin, he needs your forgiveness too. I think you are withholding yourself from him because of guilt and bitterness and it's time you gave all that up to God."

Christa wept her way through a prayer of forgiveness. When she had finished, I suggested that she go home and tell Kevin that she'd been holding unforgiveness in her heart.

"Tell him you've forgiven him, and ask him to forgive you for your part in the past. Then leave it with God, and don't allow yourself to feel guilt ever again. Remember, God has removed your sins from you as far as the east is from the west!"

Some months later, I saw Christa again. "Oh, Vickie, thank you so much for your words. You know, I wouldn't tell anyone else this," her eyes glowed with warmth as she spoke, "but Kevin and I have fallen in love all over again. And, believe it or not, our sex life is better than ever!"

Sex. We see it. We hear about it. We discuss it. We are surrounded by it. Sometimes we are attracted to it. Sometimes we are repelled by it. Difficulties with sex, along with financial problems, are the primary causes of marital discord. And considering all of the perversions and distortions our society has created, I suppose everybody has at least one misconception about it. Now, as never before, there is a vital need for us to have clear values and a grasp of both "the good news and the bad news" about human sexuality.

If we women are to help each other, we must be able to share an accurate biblical view of sex. In this area especially, we must be careful not to communicate impressions and attitudes based on our own experiences or upbringing if they are not in line with Scripture.

An Ancient Lesson in Love

There wasn't a lot said about sex in church when I was a young woman. In those days, the Song of Solomon was discussed only as an allegory relating to Christ and His church. We didn't see it literally as an eloquent poem describing the actual physical relationship between a husband and his wife. Even less did we understand that this very romantic book was God's way of communicating to us His delight in the wonderful relationship between a man and a woman in marriage.

There are some fascinating principles about biblical, marital love written across the ancient pages of the Song of Solomon. They still provide us with valuable insights into sexuality that remain apropos, even as we approach the twenty-first century.

The first lesson we learn is that *biblical love is mutual*, and represents equality to both man and woman. The bride, the "Shulammite" wasn't very self-confident.

> Do not stare at me because I am dark,
>   because I am darkened by the sun.
>
> Song of Solomon 1:6

She said, "I am dark and not very attractive." But her lover kept reinforcing her—he thought she was beautiful and told her so.

> How beautiful you are, my darling!
>   Oh, how beautiful!
>
> Song of Solomon 1:15

And how did she see him? She thought he was magnificent.

> How handsome you are, my lover!
>   Oh, how charming!
>
> Song of Solomon 1:16

Each one admired the other.

Furthermore, in the song there is no passive partner—each reaches out in passion to the other. The man says,

> Come with me from Lebanon, my bride. . . .
> How delightful is your love.
>
> Song of Solomon 4:8, 10

And the woman encourages the man,

> Come, my lover, let us go to the countryside,
>   let us spend the night in the villages.
> Let us go early to the vineyards . . .
>   there I will give you my love.
>
> Song of Solomon 7:11–12

Sexual invitations came from both man and woman. There was mutual interest, mutual desire, and mutual enticement. This is particularly interesting in the context of King Solomon's world, where a woman was generally considered to be nothing more than a possession. In the Song of Solomon, however, we get a different picture. Here, reflecting God's intention, we see sexuality acted out as a totally mutual pleasure.

Song of Solomon shows us that *biblical love is exclusive*. It is a covenant relationship for life. The woman says, "I am my lover's and my lover is mine." There is security and identification with each other. Throughout history, the marriage ceremony has been important. That's because wedding vows are said in covenant language, promising a lifetime commitment before God and all those who are witnesses.

Song of Solomon demonstrates that *biblical love is total*, encompassing both sex and friendship. "This is my lover," the woman tenderly said, "and this is my friend." Men and women are to love physically, emotionally, and spiritually. We don't marry a "great body" or a "hunk," but a person. Our culture's emphasis today on external appearances has been very damaging to the way we value one another.

Finally, we learn from this exceptional book that *biblical love is beautiful*. The poem is breathtaking in its imagery, "You are a garden locked up, my sister, my bride" (Song of Solomon 4:12). Here the husband was speaking of his bride's virginity. "You are a spring enclosed, a sealed fountain." The word fountain is used to speak of the organs that produce life in both the male and the female.

> I have come into my garden, my sister, my bride;
>   I have gathered my myrrh with my spice.
> I have eaten my honeycomb and my honey;
>   I have drunk my wine and my milk.
>
> Song of Solomon 5:1

The marriage has been consummated, and it has been a joyous, deeply satisfying union.

Following this we read a brief expression of God's invitation for all men and women to enjoy marital sex. "Eat, O friends, and drink; drink your fill, O lovers." Sexuality is to bring satisfaction. It is to be thoroughly enjoyed. It is to be celebrated.

Finally, in 8:6–7, lies the literary high point of the book.

> Place me like a seal over your heart,
>   like a seal on your arm;
> for love is as strong as death,
>   its jealousy unyielding as the grave.
> It burns like blazing fire,
>   like a mighty flame.
> Many waters cannot quench love;
>   rivers cannot wash it away.
> If one were to give
>   all the wealth of his house for love,
>   it would be utterly scorned.

A Perfect Union

Physical love in marriage, symbolically uniting two personalities by the outward act of sexual intercourse, is beautiful in the eyes of God. And it is holy. In the New Testament we read,

> "For this reason a man will leave his father and mother and be united to his wife, and the two will become one flesh." This is a profound mystery—but I am talking about Christ and the church.
>
> Ephesians 5:31–32

Sexual union, when lovingly consummated and mutually satisfying, is God's way of demonstrating a great spiritual truth. The relationship is specifically designed to illustrate God's unending love for His people. Therefore, sexual intercourse must be experienced within the framework of a permanent, giving commitment. Because of what it represents, we must not distort it and take it out of its proper place of honor.

Throughout the Bible, sexual love between man and woman is esteemed.

> May your fountain be blessed,
>   and may you rejoice in the wife of your youth.

A loving doe, a graceful deer,—
may her breasts satisfy you always,
may you ever be captivated by her love.

Proverbs 5:18–19

Marriage should be honored by all, and the marriage bed kept pure.

Hebrews 13:4

Sexuality vs. Spirituality?

Somewhere along the way, have you picked up the idea that sex is not compatible with spirituality? One woman told me rather piously, "The more I grow in my Christian faith, the less interested I am in sex."

Another concerned young woman came to me several years ago and said, "All the time I was growing up it was 'No, no, no!' Then I got married and all of a sudden it was 'Yes! yes!' I haven't been able to make the switch, and I've been married five years."

What has helped her and many other women like her is a realistic contemplation of God's Word and a commitment to living life His way.

Now for the matters you wrote about: It is good for a man not to marry. But since there is so much immorality, each man should have his own wife, and each woman her own husband. The husband should fulfill his marital duty to his wife, and likewise the wife to her husband. The wife's body does not belong to her alone but also to her husband. In the same way, the husband's body does not belong to him alone but also to his wife. Do not deprive each other except by mutual consent and for a time, so that you may devote yourself to prayer. Then come together again so that Satan will not tempt you because of your lack of self-control. I say this as a concession, not as a command. I wish that all men were as I am. But each man has his own gift from God; one has this gift, another has that.

1 Corinthians 7:1–7

This is the definitive New Testament passage about the marriage relationship. The Corinthians were an extremely dissolute society. In fact, to be called a "Corinthian" meant that you were totally immoral. It implied that you were a sort of Hugh Hefner of the day—a playboy.

So when Corinthians became converted to Christianity, the new believers had a lot of questions. And one of their biggest problems was in the area of sexuality. Because sexual depravity had always been so much a part of their lives, it was very difficult for them to understand just exactly how to change their behavior.

Some, whether married or not, were concluding that celibacy was really their best option. There were people saying that it was really much more spiritual to abstain from sex, even within marriage. Some of them were actually putting celibacy on a higher plain than marriage.

The source of that perspective was a Greek philosophy called dualism. Dualism claims that the body is bad and the spirit is good. Since sex has to do with the body and anything connected with the body is bad, therefore sex is bad. Of course this is a false belief. The Christian believer's body, soul, and spirit all belong to the Lord.

Two Valuable Gifts

Paul therefore taught in 1 Corinthians 7 that either celibacy or marriage is acceptable. Neither is more spiritual than the other because each is a gift. One person may have the gift of celibacy. Another may receive the gift of marriage. Either one is a good gift. Paul wrote,

> Because of the present crisis, I think that it is good for you to remain as you are.
>
> 1 Corinthians 7:26

Apparently, the church was going through some heavy persecution and Paul was saying, "For the time being, don't change your present status. If you get married you'll have a spouse and possibly children to worry about." His words, however, were related to a temporary crisis, and weren't intended to apply forever.

Instead he taught that, in light of so much sexual immorality, every man should have his own wife and each woman her own husband. The prevention of immorality is an extremely important reason for marriage. If a person is not married and does not have a way to legitimately satisfy his sexual needs, he is tempted in all kinds of ways.

Paul recognizes that the sex drive is powerful. He says, "If they cannot control themselves, they should marry, for it is better to marry than to burn with passion." As we consider this issue, above all else we need to grasp the reality that God created us as sexual beings.

If you happen to have a very strong need in this area, that doesn't make you an unspiritual person. The way you handle your sexuality, however, will be determined by your spirituality. If God indicates that you are to remain single or if He has taken your mate from you, He will provide you with the ability to handle your desires. You can trust Him to help you. But there's nothing shameful about a dynamic sexual drive. God made us sexual beings. Marriage has been provided to satisfy such needs, and every scriptural prohibition has to do with sexual activity outside marriage. Don't let anyone tell you the Bible prohibits sex or represses your sexuality.

Men and Marriage

George Gilder, in his book, *Men and Marriage*, asserts that having a normal, stable married life not only prevents sexual immorality, it also deters a lot of other problems. For example, says Gilder,

> A single man's aggressive tendencies, stemming from his sexual drive, are often unbridled and can be potentially destructive. Men commit over 90% of major crimes of violence, 100% of rapes, 95% of burglaries. They comprise 94% of

drunken drivers, 70% of suicides, 91% of offenders against families and children. More specifically, the chief perpetrators are single men. Single men comprise between 80% and 90% of the violators in most social and criminal offenses.

On the average, single men also earn less money than any other group in society, simply because they have less motivation. Any insurance actuary will tell you that single men are also less responsible about their bills, their driving and other personal conduct. Together with the disintegration of the family, they constitute our leading social problem.

Conversely, when a man falls in love with a woman, normally his natural responses make him want to protect and provide for her. His sexual passions are channeled, his selfish impulses are inhibited, and he discovers a sense of pride in being able to take care of his wife and his children. The marriage relationship not only discourages immorality, but a lot of other social ills as well.

Mutual Need, Mutual Satisfaction

And, as Paul describes it, the marriage relationship is reciprocal. The husband should fulfill his marital duties to the wife, and likewise the wife to the husband (1 Cor. 7:3).

In Paul's day, this kind of thinking was revolutionary. A woman had no rights in that society. Just as in the time of Solomon, she was nothing but property, available to meet her husband's needs. Christianity came in like a hurricane and blew away the old pattern, which had been the result of sin and was not part of God's original design. In God's economy, there is total sexual equality.

There is also equivalent need. Paul taught that a woman was to have her own husband and a man was to have his own wife. This implies that either sex can be tempted and has legitimate needs provided for only in marriage. Of course, we know that there is a difference in the way those needs are felt and expressed. Each partner must be sensitive to the needs of the other one and make time to meet those needs.

Paul makes another important point. He says that the wife's body does not belong to her alone but also to her husband. In the same sense, the husband's body does not belong to him alone but also to his wife. Do you see how revolutionary this was? The words translated "does not belong to" actually mean "to have rights over."

Sometimes a husband will say, "Do you see that verse? That means that you have to do it any time I want it!" Sorry, sir. That's not what Paul is telling us. He is describing loving availability to each other, which includes sensitivity to each other's needs without selfish exploitation. And just as we saw so beautifully depicted in the Song of Solomon, here we find again freedom of expression for both man and woman. Women are free to take the initiative, free to be active and not just passive partners. There is no hint in either the Old or the New Testament that sexual intercourse was intended exclusively for male pleasure!

There may be times when there must be abstinence in marriage for reasons of health or other extenuating circumstances. But verse 5 makes it clear that this is not to be a unilateral decision. It's very likely that a couple can agree to a temporary abstinence to concentrate on prayer and spiritual matters. But the warning is there that this is to be only for a limited time, mutually agreed upon. You can't come to your husband with a great revelation from God, such as, "I had my quiet time this morning and God told me that we can't have sex for six months."

And this brings to mind another area of misunderstanding. Women should not use sex as a weapon. Oh, I know it's very tempting. Sometimes we do have to get their attention, don't we? But it's not wise in the long run to use sexual relations either as a weapon or a reward.

Actually, most of us have a difficult time responding sexually when we're angry and upset, particularly if the problem hasn't yet been resolved. This is true because most women really love with their whole being while most men seem to be more compartmentalized. Your husband may not even like you on a given day, but he probably will manage to maintain his interest in the sexual relationship anyway.

Ephesians 4:26 says, 'In your anger do not sin: Do not let the sun go down while you are still angry.' Between married couples, there is an especially good reason for this teaching, because unresolved anger festers into bitterness and affects the intimacy of marriage.

Throughout the Bible, there is mutual submission in all areas related to sex. There is no headship in bed and no exploitation. On the contrary, selfish withholding violates our mutual ministry to each other.

Single and Satisfied

Marriage provides certain freedoms, and those of us who are married should enjoy those freedoms. On the other hand, there are other freedoms to be enjoyed in being single.

> I would like you to be free from concern. An unmarried man is concerned about the Lord's affairs—how he can please the Lord. But a married man is concerned about the affairs of this world—how he can please his wife—and his interests are divided. An unmarried woman or virgin is concerned about the Lord's affairs: Her aim is to be devoted to the Lord in both body and spirit. But a married woman is concerned about the affairs of this world—how she can please her husband. I am saying this for your own good, not to restrict you, but that you may live in a right way in undivided devotion to the Lord.
>
> 1 Corinthians 7:32–35

What are the advantages of the single life? If you don't have a family, you are in a unique position to be wholeheartedly devoted to the Lord. Your time and money can be given to the Lord. The single life provides a wonderful opportunity to develop a relationship with God and to serve Him. Think about some of the unmarried women that have served the Lord so outstandingly. Henrietta Mears. Amy Carmichael. My own sister, Helene Ashker, has accomplished splendid things for God as a single woman ministering to women around the world as a staff person with the Navigators.

Let's do away with the mindset that marriage is better, or that singleness is holier. Whatever you are, whatever gift God has given you, He wants to use you in a mighty way. You need only be willing to say, "Lord, my whole aim in life is to serve you." Singles have tremendous opportunities. God can give you the ability to be fruitful, joyful, and contented as a single woman.

In a world where there are more women than men, somebody is not going to be married. If your prayer is "Lord, I just want to get married; that is all I want," and you don't give God veto power, you may be setting yourself up for a real heartache.

The prayer, "Heavenly Father, I don't want to be married as much as I want your will," may have a hard time finding its way through your lips. But it is the best request a single woman could ever make. And don't stop there! Go on to say, "If it is Your will that I should marry, You send the man that You have chosen and I will wait until he gets here. I am not going to just wait in limbo, just existing, either. I am going to be vigorous. I am going to be active. I am going to grow spiritually. I am going to grow personally. I am going to grow intellectually. I am going to be a person who cares for other people. So Lord, when You're ready, You send the one You want for me. I'll be waiting, but I'll be busy!"

God does wonderful, amazing things when we have that kind of an attitude. But He expects us to do our part to maintain personal purity.

An Appeal for Purity

"Everything is permissible for me"—but not everything is beneficial. "Everything is permissible for me"—but I will not be mastered by anything. "Food for the stomach and the stomach for food"—but God will destroy them both. The body is not meant for sexual immorality, but for the Lord, and the Lord for the body. By his power God raised the Lord from the dead, and he will raise us also. Do you not know that your bodies are members of Christ himself? Shall I then take the members of Christ and unite them with a prostitute? Never! Do you not know that he who unites himself with a prostitute is one with her in body? For it is said, "The two will become one flesh." But he who unites himself with the Lord is one with Him in spirit.

Flee from sexual immorality. All other sins a man commits are outside his body, but he who sins sexually sins against his own body. Do you not know that your body is a temple of the Holy Spirit, who is in you, whom you have received from God? You are not your own; you were bought at a price. Therefore honor God with your body.

1 Corinthians 6:12–20

We've already considered the depravity of Corinth's culture. So if any of you are tempted to say, "Well, purity is just too hard these days," remember that it was just as difficult then.

The Christians at Corinth had an attitude that some of today's Christians seem to share. They believed that because they were "free in the Lord," they were free to do anything they wanted. Let me assure you that this is not true. We are only free to do good. We are only free *not* to sin. The moment we step outside the circle of God's revealed will, we are *not* free to choose the consequences. So that's not real freedom, is it? Paul addressed this issue as an abuse of Christian liberties. And that's exactly what it was.

Some Corinthians were saying, "Sex is an appetite; sex is like hunger. And you have to take care of it. If you are hungry you have to eat; if you are thirsty you have to drink. So if you feel a sexual need you have to satisfy it or else you will be starved emotionally or psychologically or even physically." In considering sex as a mere appetite, they were denying the wonderful purposes God gave it: oneness, parenthood, pleasure, and the prevention of immorality.

Obviously, we can't decide that we like the pleasure part and forget about the rest. Surrounding the purposes for sex is the wall of protection called marriage. Once marriage is removed from the equation, we are left with a separate appetite, the sex drive, that cries out for satisfaction.

The believers at Corinth were also accepting the false philosophy of dualism—that the body is evil and the spirit is good. Some of them, as we mentioned before, adopted celibacy because of this belief in dualism. Others felt, since the body is evil anyway, then it doesn't matter what it does. In 1 Thessalonians 5:23 Paul prayed:

> May God himself, the God of peace, sanctify you through and through. May your whole spirit, soul and body be kept blameless at the coming of our Lord Jesus Christ.

There is no dualism in Scripture. You were saved as a total person, not just your spirit and your soul, but also your body.

Four Pertinent Questions

Paul poses four questions that we should ask ourselves when weighing our behavior. The first, *Is this good for me?* Even if you are free to do it, is it good for you? For instance, suppose you say, "It's okay to get involved physically. A little necking won't hurt, and I know when to stop." Is it really good for you? Is it going to help you, or is it going to lower your defenses?

The second question is, *Will this control me?* Boy, is that a biggie! When we stimulate an appetite it can become controlling. And the more we feed it, the more controlling it gets. But there is a good side to this, too. We usually think of habits as being bad, and of bad things as being addictive. Romans 6:16–18 tells us that we can develop good habits, and righteousness can become addictive, too.

Don't you know that when you offer yourself to someone to obey him as slaves, you are slaves to the one whom you obey—whether you are slaves to sin, which leads to death, or to obedience, which leads to righteousness? But thanks be to God that, though you used to be slaves to sin, you wholeheartedly obeyed the form of teaching to which you were entrusted. You have been set free from sin and have become slaves to righteousness.

Third, Paul wants us to ask, *Is God seen through my body?* He says, "The body is not meant for sexual immorality, but for the Lord." When you look at this passage you have to think in terms of all the other Scripture on the same subject, stating that we are to glorify God in our bodies.

Glorify is a big, vague word, but it simply indicates that when people look at us and at our activities they should be able to see God. For us to indulge in sexual immorality and still to think that God is being seen in us is an absolute contradiction.

It is not just our spirits but our bodies which are members of Christ. And with that in mind, Paul is saying that it is inconceivable to unite immorally with someone else. When you have sexual intercourse outside the protection of marriage, Jesus is there. You are taking a member of His body, which He owns, and using it to sin. That's a pretty serious thought! And it should shock us.

The fourth pertinent question Paul asks is, *Is the Lord for my body?* The answer is a resounding yes!

God gives His Holy Spirit to live in the body of each person who has trusted Jesus Christ. He is there to give us a new power over temptation and sin. God is for us. He knows our weakness and He is there to control our sexuality if we yield that area to Him. He loves us and He knows that purity is vital to physical, mental, emotional, and spiritual health. He is on our side and will make us strong.

It's very important to emphasize the benefits of this great gift of sex that God has given us. Sex is so good that we must not spoil it by separating it from the framework God gave it—marriage. In marriage it's to be enjoyed and celebrated. Outside of marriage, it is prohibited.

Your Maker, Your Husband

Consider this if you are widowed, divorced, or single and have never been married: Isaiah 54:5 says, "For your Maker is your husband—the Lord Almighty is his name." Even those who have ideal marriages (and I haven't yet met anybody who has it all together in that area) find that there are several areas in which a husband does not meet every need.

Unhappily married women most certainly need to consider the Lord's willingness to be their husband. Instead of saying, "I have got to find someone else," or "He is such a loser," or "I am not satisfied," we have to say, "Lord, where he does not meet my needs, I'm trusting You to meet my needs."

> I know what it is to be in need, and I know what it is to have plenty. I have learned the secret of being content in any and every situation, whether well fed or hungry, whether living in plenty or in want. I can do everything through him who gives me strength.
>
> Philippians 4:12–13

I think we all must discover Paul's great secret. We have to learn it because it isn't something that just comes naturally. Isn't it wonderful to say, "Lord, You have placed me here, and You have the ability to keep me pure and fruitful and happy and productive—no matter what"?

Run, Don't Walk

Do you notice that Paul says to flee sexual immorality? Why do you think he doesn't tell us to resist it? Because it's too *hard* to resist! Run like crazy. Run like Joseph did. Joseph even left his coat in the hands of the woman who was trying to seduce him rather than stay in her house one more minute (Genesis 39). Be as drastic as necessary to physically separate yourself from temptation.

There are numerous reasons to flee immorality, and the first one is that you sin against your own body. You may think that you are satisfying something, but the one person you're really hurting is yourself. And, almost without exception, the woman is hurt the most. She is the one who may get pregnant. She may have an abortion or go through the heartaches of giving up her child for adoption or raising it alone.

The second reason to flee sexual lust is that you are the Holy Spirit's home. Paul says:

> Your body is a temple of the Holy Spirit.
>
> 1 Corinthians 6:19

This means that He is with you all the time and you are His dwelling place.

> It is God's will that you should be sanctified: that you should avoid sexual immorality; that each of you should learn to control his own body in a way that is holy and honorable, not in passionate lust like the heathen, who do not know God; and that in this matter no one should wrong his brother or take advantage of him.
>
> 1 Thessalonians 4:3–6

When considering sexual sin, we have to keep in mind the fact that we don't belong to ourselves. When Jesus Christ died on the cross and poured out His blood to pay for our sins, He redeemed us. The word *redeem* means to be bought back. As God's possession, we cannot decide, "I'm going to please God in every way except my sex life. In that area I am going to please myself." We don't have that option because every part of us belongs to God.

> But among you there must not even be a hint of sexual immorality, or of any kind of impurity, or of greed, because these are improper for God's holy people. Nor should there be obscenity, foolish talk or coarse joking, which are our of place, but rather thansgiving. For of this you can be sure: No immoral,

impure or greedy person—such a man is an idolater—has any inheritance in the kingdom of Christ and of God. Let no one deceive you with empty words, for because of such things God's wrath comes on those who are disobedient. Therefore do not be partakers with them.

For you were once darkness, but now you are light in the Lord. Live as children of light . . . and find out what pleases the Lord. Have nothing to do with the fruitless deeds of darkness, but rather expose them. For it is shameful even to mention what the disobedient do in secret.

Ephesians 5:3–12

Let's look at this very practically for a moment. We mustn't even for a moment exempt ourselves from the possibility of sexual temptation. The Scripture says, "So, if you think you are standing firm, be careful that you don't fall!" (1 Cor. 10:12).

As with most enticements, the minute you think you're safe from sexual temptation, you open yourself up to trouble. And it's when we have our eyes focused upon ourselves that we are the most vulnerable.

You and I must predetermine for purity. Don't wait until you are facing an explosive situation to weigh the issue. If you've chosen purity for yourself, you are going to be careful about all kinds of things. That's the way to avoid getting caught in a trap.

Avoiding Some Pitfalls

What are some of the traps we may face? Well, for one thing, if it is shameful to mention "what the disobedient do in secret," is it okay to watch it on television? Or at the movies? We are being conditioned to accept immoral standards and have to isolate ourselves from our culture's sexual brainwashing.

What about the way we dress? Just exactly what are we advertising when our skirts are too short or our necklines too deep? The New Testament encourages us to dress modestly, and not to draw attention to ourselves with extremes in our clothing, hair styles, or jewelry (1 Pet. 3:3–4; 1 Tim. 2:9).

We are also warned not to allow our minds to wander into areas of sexual fantasy and lust. If you begin to daydream about someone else's husband, or if you are married and start thinking about a man who isn't your spouse, you are taking a dangerous step toward adultery.

Jesus made it very clear that evil begins in the mind (Mark 7:21–23). And we already know about Satan's weapons—the lust of the flesh, the lust of the eye, and the pride of life. All of these are active in sexual temptation.

Debbie was an attractive, brown-eyed brunette, around thirty years old. She had never married and was beginning to experience a nagging fear that she would always live alone, and that her dream of being a mother would never come true.

When she met Ben, her hopes soared. Here he was at last—the exciting, energetic man of her dreams. He was handsome, with sparkling blue eyes, and he had his own business. Granted, he wasn't making a lot of money, but she admired his courage and determination. Besides, Ben treated her warmly and affectionately from the beginning, and was delightfully complimentary. Debbie, for the first time in years, felt hope—for herself and for her future.

The phone, silent for so long, began to ring two or three times a day.

"Hello, Debbie?" Her heart pounded every time she heard his voice. She could hardly believe her good fortune.

"Ben! How are you?"

"I'm terrific. I just wanted to say 'hi' and to hear your voice."

Debbie was deeply touched by Ben's calls, which often ended with his warm voice saying, "You know, I think you're wonderful, and I just wanted you to know."

Ben's affectionate ways soon led Debbie into the bedroom. The relationship was consummated with little debate—Debbie wanted to keep the affection in her life that she had long and desperately craved. And common sense told her that if Ben didn't find gratification with her, he would find it elsewhere. Besides, Ben was quite a lover, and some of her most private fantasies were coming true. She was beginning to feel like "a real woman."

But gradually, as weeks and months passed by, Ben's affectionate behavior began to change. He was often preoccupied with business concerns, and this troubled Debbie. The phone calls persisted, but with a different focus.

"Hello, Deb? Look, I need some advice. I've got to come up with $3,000 by the end of the month to cover a balloon payment. Any idea where I could borrow it?"

Debbie could hear the stress in his voice, and it saddened her. She missed his warm, personal calls, but was understanding enough to realize that he had more pressing matters to deal with at the moment.

After several days of hearing about the money crunch he was facing, Debbie came to the rescue. When he arrived at her house one Thursday night, she had a $3,000 cashier's check waiting for him—all but $250 of her savings account.

When they made love that night, he seemed like his old self. *It was worth it!* Debbie smiled to herself.

Months turned into years. Ben borrowed, paid back portions of his loans, then borrowed again. By now Debbie was glad to do his laundry twice a week—he was so busy and disorganized, and she felt valuable to him.

But Debbie was troubled by the fact that, although their sex life continued to be somewhat satisfying, the sweet affection she'd first felt from Ben was a thing of the past. He rarely complimented her, in fact he usually talked about himself. Worst of all, he never mentioned marriage.

The more she thought about it, the more distressed Debbie became. She had given her all to this man. Why didn't he love her enough to marry her?

Debbie was a Christian. She had rationalized her behavior with Ben because she loved him and had every intention of marrying him—just as soon as he asked.

Unfortunately he never did.

It took Debbie more than a year to separate herself from Ben, to recover from the rejection she felt, and to start her life over, a little older and a great deal wiser.

"God's rules make sense, Vickie," she told me not long ago, with tears in her eyes. "I think God's rules about sex can protect us from all kinds of hurt and disappointment—if we'd only follow them."

A lot of women could use a lot more wisdom in their dating relationships. I am always amazed when young women tell me that they've met a guy and he's shown a little interest, so they've started washing his laundry and making his meals. I say to them, "Listen, a guy wants to be a hunter. He doesn't want someone who is going to drop like a ripe apple into his lap."

Women need to retain a little sense of mystery. After fifteen years of affairs, a woman wrote to Ann Landers,

> I now realize that men are always ready and eager to have sex (great revelation!!). I don't believe most of them intentionally hurt or exploit women, but if a woman is too willing and too eager to please, a man finds it difficult to believe that a woman could want more from him than just a good time in bed.
>
> It has taken a long time, but I am finally willing to admit that our mothers and grandmothers weren't just prudes, they were smart. In their day couples went through a courtship or dating period that enabled them to get to know each other before becoming sexually involved. I am sure they saved a lot of pain and grief and this made for stable and lasting relationships.
>
> It is up to the woman to have enough self-respect and self-control to set limits, and to decide for herself if and when she wants to say yes.

And of course my advice is, "Say NO until you have the wedding band on."

It's Never Too Late

Maybe you're sadly thinking, "It's too late for me . . ." Well, it is never too late. Jesus Christ died for every sin that can ever be committed. There is no sin He did not pay for. If you have never trusted Christ as Savior and guilt is weighing down upon you, turn it over to Him. He's already taken the punishment. There are consequences that you will have to face—perhaps you already are facing them. But Jesus Christ took your eternal punishment, and through Him you can have forgiveness and a relationship with God.

If you are a believer and you have been involved in immorality, confess it and accept God's forgiveness. First John 1:9 says, "If we confess our sins, He is faithful and just and will forgive us our sins and purify us from all unrighteousness."

Sometimes we get so overwhelmed by our guilt that we just keep confessing and confessing. Don't do it any longer! No matter what the sin—adultery, lust, abortion, homosexuality—confess it for the last time. And don't ever bring it up to God again, because He has forgotten it (Heb. 10:17). He no longer holds you accountable for forgiven sin.

If you're single, society may try to tell you that sexuality apart from marriage is all right. Your personal history may tell you that you've fallen before and you're bound to fall again. Your physical body may tell you that you have a desperate hunger that must be met. But God's Word calls us to holiness, to purity, and to patience and trust while He supplies our needs, in His way and in His time.

Marriage and marital love were God's best gifts to man and woman in their sinless state. And they are still His greatest blessings. Marriage is a picture of God's unconditional love for His people. It is supposed to be permanent and unalterable. Once we begin to understand God's view of marriage, we will receive it as the precious provision He always intended it to be. And we won't cleave together as long as we both shall love. We will cleave to each other as long as we both shall live.

5

The Truth About Submission

*L*ana was a starry-eyed newlywed, passionately in love with her new husband. Not two years before, she had been through a painful divorce. *This time it's going to work, no matter what it takes,* she told herself time and again. The failure of her first marriage haunted her. *This time I'll do everything his way, and nothing will go wrong.*

She and Jeff were both Christians. Although they attended a small fellowship, they had no close Christian friends. They had been married just six weeks when Lana began to feel sick. Her breasts were painfully sore, and she was constantly nauseous and sleepy.

I wonder if I'm pregnant . . .

The thought brought horror to Lana's heart. Jeff had made it very clear that he wanted no children for at least five years. Even after that, he wasn't so sure. "You're all I need," he'd told Lana. "I don't need any other friends, and I sure don't need kids."

But the pregnancy test she'd secretly purchased at the pharmacy confirmed her worst fears. Yes, Lana was pregnant. And she was terrified. What would Jeff say?

"Well, we'll just have to see about an abortion," he told her matter-of-factly when she finally found the courage to break the news to him.

"Some people think abortion is, well, murder," she remarked tentatively.

"Well, that's their problem. This is my life, you're my wife, and I'm saying that you're going to have an abortion. We've got a good thing going here and we don't need to mess it up with a baby." He gave her a hug and a kiss.

Lana was saddened. She kept having brief glimpses of a baby in her mind's eye—a baby who looked a little like her and a little like Jeff. But her commitment to her new husband overshadowed all other considerations.

All her life, Lana had been taught that Christian wives are supposed to submit to their husbands' authority and wishes. In her first marriage, she'd been less than cooperative, and the marriage had ended in divorce. As far as she was concerned, she'd learned her lesson. This time she would submit to her husband's orders—no matter what.

She called the local abortion clinic number, made an appointment, and walked into the clinic the next day with Jeff. She waited tearfully and nervously for her name to be called. As Lana finally got up to go into the cubicle where the abortion would be performed, she turned to her new husband and smiled bravely.

"I hope you know how much I love you. I'd do anything for you, Jeff."

What does submission mean? How inclusive is it? Does it mean that a wife can never disagree, can never have a part in decision making, cannot control the budget, write a check, or even have money to spend without accounting for it? Does it mean that a wife obeys her husband in the same way a slave obeys his master, or the way a child obeys his parents? Does it mean that a woman's personality is to be repressed or obliterated, having no valid expression? Is marriage a chain of command?

Accepting God-Given Authority

In the first place, let's consider God's view of human authority in general.

> Everyone must submit himself to the governing authorities, for there is no authority except that which God has established. The authorities that exist have been established by God. Consequently, he who rebels against the authority is rebelling against what God has instituted, and those who do so will bring judgment on themselves.
>
> Romans 13:1–2

God has instituted human authority, and it is for our own good. First Peter 2:13 picks up the same theme. It says,

> Submit yourselves for the Lord's sake to every authority instituted among men: whether to the king, as the supreme authority, or to governors, who are sent by him to punish those who do wrong and to commend those who do right.

What does this mean? Paul and Peter are both saying that submission to God means submission to God-ordained authority. This means that rebellion against such authority is rebellion against God.

There are four major areas of authority addressed in the Bible—human government, church leadership, employers, and the home.

In the home there are two levels of authority. The first is the authority that both parents have over the children. The second is the authority that the husband has over the wife. Sometimes, when the subject of submission in the home is discussed, the wife is placed in the same relationship as the children. That should not be so.

In some churches and in some books and seminars, submission is so badly taught that women have been told to obey their husbands, even if they instruct their wives, as Jeff did Lana, to do something morally wrong.

Some Notable Exceptions

In thinking this through, I've come to realize that there are biblical exceptions to submission in every area of authority. For instance, with regard to obedience to government, the Egyptian midwives did not obey Pharaoh and kill all the little boy babies—thus Moses was saved and God blessed the midwives. Rahab did not obey her king and turn in the Hebrew spies—she and her family were spared when Jericho was destroyed. Daniel would not pray to an idol or to his king, and he deliberately disobeyed the king's decree. God honored him for his faithfulness.

As far as employer/employee relations are concerned, we read about three God-fearing young men who were administrators under Nebuchadnezzar, king of Babylon. They would not bow down in worship to his image and laid their lives on the line as a result. And God rescued them from the fiery furnace.

There was also an obscure little man named Obadiah whose story is recorded in 1 Kings 18:9–14. When all the prophets of God were ordered killed by Ahab and Jezebel, he protected a hundred of them. He was employed as a servant of the king, and yet he defied his employer's orders.

God once blessed the actions of a son who disobeyed his own father. Saul's son Jonathan was ordered by his father to kill David. Instead he protected David, who was his closest friend.

And as for wifely submission, consider the story of Abigail. Her husband Nabal had arrogantly decreed that David and his men should receive no provisions from his vast and wealthy household. Yet Abigail disregarded her husband's orders and did just the opposite. She delivered massive supplies to the future king and even pleaded with him not to retaliate against her household in response to her husband's refusal to help, "because he is a fool!"

Why did Abigail do this? Because she was concerned that David, God's anointed king, not bloody his hands over her husband's churlish behavior. Because she was protecting her husband's life. And because she was saving the lives of all the men in her household.

Abigail was rewarded richly for her efforts. God struck down her foolish husband Nabal. David, the recipient of her generosity, was profoundly impressed by her wisdom and courage. Once she was widowed, he took her to be his wife.

Clearly, human authority can be abused. And as children of God, we must obey our Father. The apostles have set a vivid example for us.

The religious leaders of Israel, called the Sanhedrin, were supposed to be obeyed, and every good Jew obeyed them. Even if the men in the Sanhedrin were wrong, they were to be honored and respected. The Sanhedrin decided that the apostles could not teach about Jesus Christ.

Look at Acts 4:18–19.

> Then they called them in again and commanded them not to speak or teach at all in the name of Jesus. But Peter and John replied, "Judge for yourselves whether it is right in God's sight to obey you rather than God. For we cannot help speaking about what we have seen and heard."

In Acts 5:28–29 the Sanhedrin's high priest again rebuked them,

> "We gave you strict orders not to teach in this name," he said. "Yet you have filled Jerusalem with your teaching and are determined to make us guilty of this man's blood."
>
> Peter and the other apostles replied: "We must obey God rather than men!"

Obedience to God

We are not free to cop-out on responsibility by doing something wrong because an authority tells us to do it. All human authority is under the umbrella of God's authority, and God's authority must be obeyed first. You can't say "Well, my boss told me to lie and I have to lie because he is my boss," or, like Lana in our story, "I have to do this because my husband told me to." No, you don't have to!

If there is a conflict between God's rules and man's, the believer must choose to obey God. And bear in mind, there may be suffering involved. Of course we know, as 1 Peter 2:19 tells us, if we suffer for doing good, God is pleased with us.

Submission is not mindless, childlike obedience without responsibility for one's actions. So what is it? Whenever submission of the wife is taught in the New Testament, the headship of the husband is equally taught. It is a two-way street. Let's contemplate the husband-wife relationship, that very unique union which is so different from every other kind of authority/submission relationship.

In Ephesians 5:18–21, we learn that all Christians, men and women alike, are to be controlled by the Spirit of God. One of the evidences of the Spirit's control is submission to one another out of reverence for Christ. This kind of Christian submission is only possible if we are being controlled by the Spirit.

Who is doing the submitting in Ephesians 5:21? Everybody! It is a mutual submission. As Spirit-filled Christians we are to submit to one another. Then Paul goes on to be more specific. In the verses that follow, he describes how that submission looks in various categories. He talks about parents and children. Slaves and masters. Husbands and wives.

> Wives, submit to your husbands as to the Lord. For the husband is the head of the wife as Christ is the head of the church, his body, of which he is the Savior. Now as the church submits to Christ, so also wives should submit to their husbands in everything.
>
> Husbands, love your wives just as Christ loved the church and gave himself up for her to make her holy, cleansing her by

the washing with water through the word, and to present her to himself as a radiant church, without stain or wrinkle or any other blemish, but holy and blameless. In this same way, husbands ought to love their wives as their own bodies. He who loves his wife, loves himself.

Ephesians 5:22–28

Submission vs. Obedience

How does "submit to your husbands" differ from Genesis 3:16 where God says your husband "will rule over you"? Are the two passages talking about the same thing? No, in fact they are quite different. The Genesis prediction comes as the consequence of sin. The Ephesians' imperative comes as the result of our being filled with the Spirit. The two are not the same at all.

First of all, let's talk about the word "submit." This is a different term from the word "obey," which is used in relation to children and slaves. It is important for us to understand that the word used to command obedience from children and slaves is never used in a command form for wives. The "submission" Paul applies to husbands and wives can be compared to the relationship between a president and a vice-president. They are equal in personhood, but they have different responsibilities. Since the president has greater authority, he also has greater responsibilities. This is true in marriage as well. God holds the husband responsible to love his wife and be a godly leader.

Paul says "submit" or "subject yourself" to your husband. Peter says "to your own husband." That eliminates the possibility of women being submissive to all men, a fallacy which is sometimes taught in Christian circles. Neither does it mean that single women must submit to single men.

Submit to your own husband as to the Lord—that is the command. So does your husband somehow become the Lord in your eyes? Should you submit to him unquestioningly just as if he were God? No! The Scripture simply means that you

submit to your husband's leadership as an act of obedience to
Jesus Christ. Do you see the difference? You obey Jesus Christ
by your voluntary submission to your husband.

This kind of submission has nothing to do with inferiority. The fact that we see it in the Godhead confirms this. The
Son submits to the Father. The Spirit submits to the Father
and the Son. Yet Father, Son, and Spirit are each called God.
There is no inferiority implied. There is simply order—the
proper order which God has designed.

This voluntary submission is also a service rendered to God
through the control of the Holy Spirit. It is not something that
we are going to do happily on our own. At one time or another, all of us are bound to resist it. But keep in mind that
while women are commanded to submit to their husbands, men
are commanded to sacrificially love their wives.

Seeking the Will of God

What we often don't realize is that there are many blessings to be found in biblical submission.

I had to learn this by hard experience. When I was married thirty-nine years ago, there was no pre-marital counseling, nor were there the numerous books and courses on
Christian marriage that we have today. My father had died
when I was seven, so I was not accustomed to male authority.

When Fred and I married, I really didn't think much
about this submission stuff. It took nine years of stubbornness
on my part and determination on my husband's before the
Lord penetrated my self-will with His Word. My husband and
I were at an impasse. I wanted to do something that he refused to have done. I was reading Ephesians 5 one day, and
the Lord clearly spoke to me from the written page. "Wives,
submit to your husbands as to the Lord. For the husband is
the head of the wife . . ."

*But Lord, what if I'm right and he's wrong? What will hap-
pen if we don't do something about this problem right away? My*

imagination projected all kinds of terrible consequences if we didn't do things my way. But the Lord kept up the pressure, and finally I said, "Lord, I am Your child and this is Your Word which I must obey. I want Your will for my life more than I want my own way. I am willing for my husband to be an instrument in Your hands to show me Your will. And I will trust You to give him the right decisions."

From then on, before I suggested a course of action to my husband, I'd tell the Lord, "It's Your will I want. My husband's decision will be Your will for this situation."

It began to amaze me how many times we were in agreement. The tension and conflict caused by my insistence on my own way disappeared as I trusted God to speak to me through my husband.

This is the approach a Christian woman can take whether she is married to an unbeliever, an immature believer, or a strong leader. When we depend on God to use the instruments He has provided for our guidance, He has a way of changing minds, wills, and actions to bring about His purposes.

I should tell you that it took a year before what I thought had to be done right away was done. And none of the dire consequences I thought would result ever happened. God understands the pressures that submission brings into our lives and He is there to help. All He wants is that we want His will above all else, even our own way. There is a wonderful freedom and peace when we view the marital relationship this way.

Marilee was the youngest of six children and had moved from New York to California to marry Ted. Most of her brothers and sisters still lived on the East Coast, as did her widowed mother. In recent months her mother's health had deteriorated dramatically.

Each of Marilee's siblings had shared the responsibility for the dying woman, financially and with physical care. Ted had been generous about sending money to New York to assist with medical bills, but he stubbornly refused to allow his wife to go care for her mother. There had been several unpleasant conversations about the subject, and Ted's final words had been, "The answer is no, and don't ask me again!"

"It's so unreasonable!" Marilee fumed as she spoke to her friend Helen. "We've got plenty of money, and Ted and the kids are perfectly capable of taking care of themselves for a few weeks. He's just being controlling, and I hate it!"

"I don't blame you at all, Marilee . . ." Helen was frustrated with Ted, too. But good friend that she was, she didn't want to fan her friend's anger into full flame.

"I feel like taking money out of the bank, buying a ticket, and just leaving. That's what I should do. What if Mom dies before I can get there? I'll never forgive myself. I haven't seen her in five years, Helen. Five years!"

"Well, before you do that, let's pray together. I think God may want to do something about this Himself."

"Like what?" Marilee was so incensed, she couldn't even imagine God being on her side in the matter.

"Like changing Ted's mind."

"Oh, sure. Right. Ted's mind? God might be able to create the universe in six days, but He'll never change Ted's mind!"

Helen shook her head and smiled. "Come on, let's pray anyway."

Reluctantly Marilee brought the whole issue before the Lord. She told Him how angry she was. Before long tears replaced her rage—grief over her mother's impending death. How she longed to see her again before she died. But then she added, "Lord, I want Your will more than my own way."

Helen hugged Marilee before the two parted. "I'm expecting a miracle, whether you are or not!"

"Well, God can do anything, I guess. But this seems pretty hopeless."

That night while Marilee was preparing dinner, Ted walked into the kitchen, and rather timidly handed her an envelope. "Marilee, I think God wants you to have this . . ."

"What is it?"

"It's a plane ticket to New York. You leave Friday, and the return date is open. I wasn't sure how long you'd need to stay. The kids and I will be fine."

Marilee stared at Ted in absolute shock. "What on earth changed your mind, Ted?"

"I don't know. I just got to thinking about how I'd feel if my own mother were sick, and I realized I was being unreasonable. Sorry, Honey." Ted grinned sheepishly. "You know how I am . . ."

This applies to unbelieving husbands, too. So don't say, "Well, my husband isn't a believer so I'm not going to submit to him." Just pray for him. Submit to him. And leave the rest with God.

Of course, *wives must submit to their husbands in everything* certainly does not refer to sin. No wife should ever submit to a dishonest or immoral plan. And even in the case of righteous or neutral decisions, from time to time we all have our own personal struggles with submission.

Remember the reason we are to submit. Because, just as Christ is the head of the church and the church is His body, so the husband is the head of the wife (Eph. 5:23).

A Special Kind of Love

When you read the passage on marital submission in Ephesians 5, you notice that much more responsibility is given to the husband than to the wife. Paul concludes his remarks by saying,

> Each one of you also must love his wife as he loves himself, and the wife must respect her husband.
>
> Ephesians 5:33

This word "love" is not that affectionate, loving friendship we find in Titus 2, where women are instructed to love their husbands. This love is the Greek word *agape*. *Agape* love is far more an act of volition than of emotion. It is a chosen attitude in which a man lays aside his own selfish desires and his own rights and takes care of his wife.

As Paul instructs husbands to love their wives, he uses the analogy, "just as Christ loved the church." How did Christ show His love for the church? Jesus Christ did not have to leave His throne in heaven. He did not have to come to earth, to live in poverty for thirty-three years in a human body. He did not have to suffer at the hands of sinful men. He did not have to die. Jesus Christ gave up His rights so that we could have eternal life. And this is the same type of love a husband is supposed to extend toward his wife.

Agape love is not dependent on the recipient. It is an act of the will. It is a commitment. "Love your wife as your own body" and because she really is an extension of your body. Here, again, the one-flesh relationship of Genesis 2 is emphasized. The wife is not a child, not a slave, not a toy, not a property. She is his complementary partner, one flesh with him. He is to nourish and cherish her just as he nourishes and cares for his own body.

Seeking Her Highest Good

Biblical marriage requires mutual submission. Yes, the wife yields her rights and submits to her husband's leadership. But the husband is to yield his rights to independence, to controlling all the money, and to making all the decisions. He is to recognize that he is married to a woman who is one flesh with him.

For some men, this is a difficult assignment and a big issue. It is very hard for a man to sacrificially give up his own rights for the sake of his wife. And yet God requires an unselfish love that seeks the woman's highest good, with no hint of her husband lording it over her. This view of marriage is distinctively Christian, an expression of God's love acted out through the control of the Spirit.

As a matter of fact, Christian marriages were astonishing to the Roman world. In a society where women had no rights, here was wifely submission balanced by loving sacrificial headship. Marriage was placed on a very firm basis of mutuality, with both partners having equal rights. Such an arrangement was revolutionary in that day.

I remember hearing a prominent leader say, "A husband's responsibility is to find out his wife's strengths and skills and to do everything he can to develop them." And this man was as good as his word. When he realized that his wife Jean was gifted at writing, he saw to it that once the children were grown, she went back to graduate school and got her degree in journalism. Today his wife is a well-known author and speaker, because her husband took it upon himself to encourage the use of her gifts and bring her to fulfillment. That is what loving, sacrificial headship can accomplish.

When comparing marriage with Christ's relationship to the church, Paul says, "This is a profound mystery." Now the word *mystery* in the Bible is not like an Agatha Christie novel or a "Perry Mason" episode on television. A mystery in the Bible is something that cannot be found out by human reasoning but must be revealed by God.

How can God take two totally opposite people and make them one? And how can Christ be wedded to the church in one body? Both are, indeed, mysteries. Do you see why Satan attacks Christian marriages? Because he wants to defile and distort the picture God has given us to illustrate His Son's relationship with the church.

Strengths and Weaknesses

Husbands, in the same way be considerate as you live with your wives, and treat them with respect as the weaker partner and as heirs with you of the gracious gift of life, so that nothing will hinder your prayers.

1 Peter 3:7

Some people have understood the expression "weaker partner" to mean that the wife is weaker physically, mentally, spiritually, and morally. This is not the case. Paul is talking solely about her physical distinctiveness. Woman was created to bear children, not to chop down trees.

It is interesting to note that a man's prayer life can be blocked if he does not respect or honor his wife. Both partners must keep grace and forgiveness alive in the marriage. When bitterness and resentment are given a place in the home, more is lost than personal warmth and enjoyment. The vital element of the husband's prayer life, through which he receives both guidance and assistance, will be hindered. No couple should attempt to function within the confines of that sort of handicap.

A man should prayerfully take his wife's concerns to heart when making any decision. He should listen to her. He should pray with her. He should seriously consider the consequences she might bear in the wake of his choices. There ought not be too many instances in a good, healthy marriage where a man actually moves in a direction of which his wife disapproves. I heard one of my professors say, "Men, if your wife doesn't agree with a major decision, don't do it. Ask God to bring her into agreement if it's His will."

Becoming a True Husband

Marriage should provide a warm and healthy environment where the wife can grow to her full potential. She should thrive under her husband's protection, encouragement, and selfless provisions.

I found some powerful insights in a book by Dwight Small called *Marriage as Equal Partnership*. It comes to us from a man's point of view and summarizes a husband's headship in a clear and eloquent manner.

Headship is not at all a husband becoming a master, boss, tyrant, authoritarian—the dominant coercive force. Neither does it imply control or restriction. His being assertive and her being suppressed. And it cannot mean he assumes any prerogatives of greater virtue, intelligence or ability. It does not mean that he is active and she is passive. He is the voice and she the silent partner. Nor does it mean that he is the tribal chief, the family manager, the one who has superior rights or privileges. He is not the decision maker, problem solver, goal setter or director of everyone else in the family's life. Rather he is primarily responsible for the common advance toward freedom and fellowship—creating a partnership of equals under one responsible head. . . . Throughout the equalitarian process the husband knows all the while that he bears the responsibility, before God, for the healthful maintenance of the marriage. . . .

We are on the safe side when we see the definition of subjection in the person of Jesus himself. He, being equal with the Father, relinquished that equality to become the servant of us all. . . . Every Christian is called to servanthood as the expression of his or her new life in Christ. Servanthood is the identifying mark of every true Christian believer. A servant's role is to make sure that the other person's needs are met.

In marriage, servanthood is an act of strength, not weakness.

6

When It's Not Ideal

I have told him a thousand times that he needs to get his life right with God. What more can I do?"

A strand of glossy auburn hair fell across Lee's eye, and she impatiently brushed it behind her ear. Expensive rings sparkled on her hands, and a large gold chain gleamed against her designer suit. When Lee and Ray got married, neither of them had been Christian believers. They had both been active in the business world, and they still enjoyed equally successful careers. Lee was executive vice president for a national ad agency. Ray was a corporate attorney.

Two years before, Lee had been led to the Lord by a woman friend, and her hunger for spiritual values had propelled her into a hectic pursuit of Bible studies, sermon tapes, and Christian music. She craved growth, and she had a genuine desire to see God's hand at work in her life. Lee's attitudes, behavior, and style had been dramatically transformed by her newfound faith.

Meanwhile, her husband was still the same old Ray—shady in his business dealings, ruthless in his contract negotiations, and vulgar in his humor and vocabulary.

The Christian faith had clearly become a stumbling block in this once happy marriage. And, aggressive as she was, Lee wasn't about to let an opportunity pass without reminding Ray that he was an infidel—in thought, word, and deed.

"I'm not afraid to tell him what I think about it; you can be sure of that!" Lee announced rather proudly.

I looked at her in amusement. "What would you think if I told you never to mention your Christian faith again?"

Without hesitation, Lee replied, "I'd say you're wrong. Jesus gave the Great Commission to all of us. We're supposed to share our faith with everyone—including our husbands."

"Lee, the Lord has some special instructions for women like you. They are simple: Pray for your husband, live a godly life in front of him, treat him with respect, and don't talk about your faith unless he asks."

"That's ridiculous! Ray will never come to God if I don't say anything. I'm the only Christian he knows. Look, Vickie, you've got to help me find a way to convince him to become a Christian. Otherwise I think our marriage is doomed. He's awful!"

Let's face it, we live in a fallen world. Sometimes we women don't measure up to God's standards. At other times, the men in our lives don't. There are wives who refuse to submit because they think it somehow makes them inferior. And there are husbands who use submission as a club to get their own way. They do not love sacrificially at all.

Lee's situation raises some very important issues. What does the Bible have to say about the profane, irreverent husband? About the selfish, irresponsible one? About the unsaved husband? About the abuser? Scripture doesn't give us an exact verse for each of these, but there are principles in the Bible which do give us guidelines. Some of these guidelines are not easy to follow. They are a challenge for us.

> Wives, in the same way, be submissive to your husbands
> so that, if any of them do not believe the word, they may be
> won over without words by the behavior of their wives, when

they see the purity and reverence of your lives. Your beauty should not come from outward adornment, such as braided hair and the wearing of gold jewelry and fine clothes. Instead, it should be that of your inner self, the unfading beauty of a gentle and quiet spirit, which is of great worth in God's sight. For this is the way the holy women of the past who put their hope in God used to make themselves beautiful. They were submissive to their own husbands, like Sarah, who obeyed Abraham and called him her master. You are her daughters if you do what is right and do not give way to fear.

1 Peter 3:1–6

Men Who Say No to God

Let me explain what this passage *doesn't* mean. First of all, it is not a promise to a Christian woman who has decided to marry an unsaved man, that her good conduct will win her husband to Christ. This passage is not a carte blanche for you to say, "I can marry anybody I want, and God will eventually save him." God's Word clearly says that the only person a believer should marry is another believer (1 Cor. 7:39; 2 Cor. 6:14).

Peter was addressing a group of new believers. When the gospel had first been presented to them, in some cases, several wives had responded in faith, but their husbands hadn't. This was a situation where both spouses were unsaved when they got married, and one had since come to know the Lord.

And another thing, if you are "unequally yoked," no matter how you got that way, you don't become the head of the home just because you are more spiritually alive. Unfortunately, this is what some women think. Peter's words really address that misconception.

Now let's look at what this passage from Peter's epistle *does* say to us. What is the spiritual equation in your home? You may not be able to talk freely about Christian things because of your husband's personality. He may be unsaved, unresponsive, difficult, or totally obstinate. He may be in a state of unbelieving disobedience. The primary reference here is to the unsaved mate. But after years of counseling women, I know all too well that some of our saved mates can be unreceptive to spiritual issues, too.

Consciously or unconsciously, some men have determined that they are not going to grow in grace any more. They are sick of Bible studies. They refuse to attend church unless they feel like it. They're telling us, either in word or action, "Okay, you can go on and on with this Christian thing, but I am going to stay right here, and I am not moving. I'm not going to become a fanatic, too!"

I believe Peter's words can pertain to Christian wives of unbelievers as well as to the wives of Christian men who are in rebellion. In either case, the same principles apply.

Trusting Him Who Judges Justly

Peter had said in the previous chapter, "Slaves submit yourself to your masters with all respect. Not only to those who are good and considerate, but also to those who are harsh." This also applies to wives because a few lines later Peter says, "Wives, *in the same way* be submissive to your husbands." Wives are to respond to difficult husbands "in the same way" that a slave was to render faithful, efficient, loyal service to a difficult master.

A slave was to obey even if his master treated him harshly while he was doing his job well. The Christian slave was to do so because he was conscious of God, and Peter used Christ as an example—the ultimate example. Jesus Christ, who was sinless, suffered unjustly and accepted unfair treatment without retaliating.

I know. We all groan inside when we hear this sort of thing. It is so easy to snap back—so easy to pay back. But do you realize that if Jesus Christ had not done what He did, none of us would know God? None of us would be forgiven. None of us would have the assurance of heaven. He suffered for redemptive reasons. And I believe that we can live in a difficult situation for redemptive purposes, too. The reason Jesus was able to bear the burden of unjust treatment was because He entrusted Himself "to him who judges justly." We can do the same.

We have a heavenly Father who knows our limits and our abilities. He esteems justice and recognizes inequity. He knows our hearts and our motives. We can commit ourselves and our cause to Him. I believe that we can both give and receive encouragement in this regard. The route is not always an escape from the situation. Sometimes the route may be one of endurance—an endurance that God enables us to live out.

A Strong, Silent Message

Peter says that unbelieving husbands may be won over without a word, without corrective conversations, simply by the behavior of their wives. A man can be changed just by observing the purity and reverence of his wife's life.

I think this is probably the hardest thing for a woman to do—to keep quiet and just let her actions speak for her. Have you ever thought, *Oh, Lord, I really want him to know this! How am I going to get it across? Let's see—I'll think of some tactful way of saying it. Maybe I can put a tape in our tapedeck. Or leave the Bible open. Or lay a tract out where he'll see it.*

Don't take on the responsibility for your husband's spiritual development. You don't need to be clever or covert. God is saying, "I know that you are limited because of the submission-leadership relationship. And I am promising you some strong help."

First of all, God wants you to know that you are not the only means by which He is able to reach this man. You aren't solely responsible. God is able to bring all kinds of other people and circumstances into the picture. He has ways of reaching out to your husband that you can't even imagine. Meanwhile, your husband can't help but observe the purity and the reverence for God in your life, an attitude which controls everything you do. Your behavior is going to make an impact on him whether you think it will or not.

Outstanding, Not Outrageous

With this in mind, begin to realize that if you want to influence your husband, you have to have a different value system than this world's. For example, you are not going to seduce him into Christianity. You have to leave behind worldly ideas and the world's approach. Tell yourself, "My outward appearance as well as my actions are going to mirror the beliefs I treasure on the inside."

I get really upset with Christian books that advocate sexual manipulation. Just remember that whatever you gain by manipulation you must maintain by manipulation. It is so much better to honestly say, "Lord, I can't do anything about his beliefs or his behavior. So I give this man into Your hands." God will bless your attitude of submission, both to your husband and to God, as a means of evangelism.

We say, "How am I going to make this man become more spiritual?"

God says, "I am going to use you to win him to Me without another word said. I am going to enable you by the spirit of God to conduct yourself in such a loving and irreproachable way that it will have an impact on him—whether he admits it or not."

What talking won't do, kindness and purity will. Peter wanted these women to understand that their beauty wasn't supposed to come merely from outward adornment. Now this doesn't mean that we can't wear jewelry. Or enjoy pretty clothes. And it doesn't mean that we shouldn't fix our hair attractively.

In those decadent Roman times, coiffures were sometimes so elaborate that a woman might need a slave to walk behind her, propping her hair up with a pole! These flamboyant coiffures were intricately adorned with jewels and gold and pearls. Peter is talking about extreme, way-out clothes. He is not talking about ordinary apparel.

Let's not get the idea, like some of the old Quakers, that Christian women should be garbed in gray and black, or that we are particularly spiritual if we look terrible. God's woman is consistent. She is attractive. She does not use extreme, outlandish sexual techniques to win her husband. She is going to have a beauty that is unfading, a beauty that comes from "a gentle and quiet spirit."

Following in Sarah's Footsteps

Meekness means controlled strength. And a woman with a meek, gentle spirit is not agitated by circumstances. She is not panicked by every new thing that comes along. She does not respond to surprises by blowing her top. Her quiet spirit flows directly from her staunch hope and trust in God. The way to win a difficult husband is to have a spirit like Jesus Christ. A spirit that is unruffled. A spirit that can face tragedy. A spirit that can deal with unwarranted suffering.

That's not to say she pretends nothing is wrong, practicing denial and refusing to admit to adversity. How can a woman cope with her troubles? Peter tells us the secret—she puts her confidence in God. She trusts Him with her life and with her husband. And notice what it says about Sarah being our example: "You are her daughters if you do what is right and do not give way to fear" (1 Pet. 3:6).

In the midst of doing right, to what are we the most vulnerable? Anxiety. Panic. Fear.

What if he gets mad at me?

Suppose he gets abusive?

Suppose he takes away some of the things I enjoy?

Through prayer and focus upon God's Word, we can entrust ourselves to God and allow Him to protect our interests.

Naturally, things don't always work out the way we want them to. I love the fact that Sarah is the example that is used (Genesis 12–23). What kind of person was Sarah? Was she a doormat? Hardly! Do you notice that every time Sarah gave her husband advice, he took it, whether it was good advice or not?

The last time that Sarah advised her husband, she told him to get rid of his son Ishmael. Abraham didn't want to do it, but God told him, "Do whatever Sarah tells you." We have a woman here who was anything but a pushover. She was not a silent partner. She was actively involved. She protected her husband. She was interested in his concerns. She was committed to his walk with God. I think it's noteworthy that God used a woman like Sarah—a woman with normal emotions, a woman who experienced deep heartache—as a role model for us.

Sarah was infertile, and knew to the depths of her soul what barrenness meant. She had experienced all of the reproach that went with it. She knew what it was to be jealous. In fact, she became violent with her servant Hagar, who was mother of Abraham's son Ishmael. God understands our feminine nature. He understands our needs as women. And in spite of her failings, He uses Sarah as an example of a holy woman, a woman set apart for God (1 Pet. 3:6).

I am so glad God didn't use someone like Ruth for this particular role model. It's much more difficult to relate to Ruth, because everything she did was good. He gave us somebody who was more like we are. And Sarah was a wonderful woman. She respected and honored Abraham, shared his dreams, and supported his walk with God.

And what happened to Sarah when her husband failed her, abandoned her to Pharaoh's harem, and lied to save his own skin? God rescued her, not once but twice, even though she'd gone along with Abraham's lie, agreeing that she was his sister. Remember, her motive was to protect her husband's life, so she cooperated with his dishonest scheme. Incidentally, don't use that as an excuse to do wrong. Sarah thought their situation was a matter of life and death.

Why Some Prayers Are Unanswered

As we noted in an earlier chapter, Peter gave the men he was addressing a warning.

> Husbands . . . be considerate as you live with your wives, and treat them with respect as the weaker partner and as heirs with you of the gracious gift of life, so that nothing will hinder your prayers.
>
> 1 Peter 3:7

He was saying, "If you don't treat your wife properly, when you pray something is going to snip your prayer off before it ever reaches heaven." Being harsh, bitter, demanding, selfish, and arrogant toward your wife will mar your fellowship with God and result in unanswered prayer.

I wonder how many prayers are unanswered right now because some men have this kind of an attitude toward their wives? By the way, I personally suspect that the woman who takes the position of "Well, I'm more spiritual than he is so I'm taking over!" is in the same danger.

No matter what, a man is not supposed to look on his wife with scorn because she doesn't happen to have the same muscle structure he has or the same hormonal makeup. And yet that is often what we see today. Even in churches we pick up that macho idea, "Isn't that just like a woman? What do you expect from a woman?"

Within the Christian community that type of woman bashing is not spiritual, and it is not biblical. And it was certainly nothing Jesus ever did. In fact, when you find the disciples railing at Mary because, in all her emotion, she wasted her precious, fragrant ointment on Jesus, He said, "Leave her alone, she has done a beautiful thing to me. And wherever the gospel is given, she will be remembered . . . she has done what she could." I think God wants each of us to treasure that assurance within our own hearts. By faith, let's believe that when we have done what we could within our circumstances, He is pleased with us.

"Heirs with you" reminds us that men and women are saved the same way. They confess that they are sinners, believe that Jesus Christ, God's Son, died in their place and trust Him alone for forgiveness and eternal life. There is no distinction. Men and women will have an equal share in the coming age. And even now we have an equal share in the grace of God in salvation and in the blessings of being in God's family.

Women, it is important for you to know, if you are living in a situation which is harsh and wrong, that God does not approve of it. It should make you feel better to know that God isn't pleased with your circumstances. Please be reassured of His concern and compassion, even if Bible verses have been misused to tell you otherwise.

It disturbs me when I hear people distort Scripture to force something God does not want. You can trust in God—He isn't against women. God isn't up there saying, "That's the way to treat them, you guys." I want you to realize that the Lord really is on your side and has promised to help you.

Is Abuse Permissible?

What about wife abuse? This isn't just happening down in some poor neighborhood across town. Sad to say, wife abuse is common even in Christian churches. The following excerpt from a *Moody Monthly* article by Chuck and Winnie Christiansen typifies the kind of advice that a woman has often received when she said, "My husband is abusive and violent. What can I do?"

Dear Chuck and Winnie:

Where in the Bible does it give my husband permission to beat me? My husband claims to be a Christian, we go to church and as far as anyone is concerned he is a wonderful guy. But at home it is another story. He has thrown me, beaten me and threatened our children; we have two small ones. I am now separated from him, but my pastor told me I should go home. He said God has called me to be an abused wife. I asked, did God call my husband to be an abuser? He is supposed to be a Christian. Where in the Bible does it tell husbands to beat their wives? The pastor replied, "That isn't the issue. The issue is that it is your place to submit." I said I couldn't accept that. I left because I feared for my life and the lives of my children. Would God want me and my children living in danger? It's my non-Christian friends who told me to leave and to start a life of my own with my children. I am confused. Can you help?

I couldn't agree more emphatically with the answer the Christiansens gave to this poor woman. They assured her that there is definitely no verse in the entire Bible which gives a husband, whether he's a believer or not, the right to abuse either his wife or his children. And to use the passages regarding marital submission as justification for such actions is heresy. Such a man is simply twisting the Bible around to endorse his violence.

Some misinformed teachers have said that Genesis 3:16 warrants either verbal or physical abuse. That is absurd. We've already learned that God's words to Eve were simply a prediction of what would happen in family relationships because of the Fall. It is unthinkable that God would direct men to dehumanize their wives or to destroy their children physically or emotionally.

We've seen, in Ephesians 5, that Paul reveals the kind of love God expects husbands to have for their wives. It is Christ's love. It is a giving, sacrificial love that causes a man to be willing to lay his life down for his spouse. God does not take lightly the abuse of any of His children, or the distortion of Scripture to support it.

Darrell was youth pastor at a large, thriving evangelical church. He was blond, boyish, and lovable. He was a wonderful storyteller with an engaging sense of humor. Charm was his middle name. Darrell, his petite wife, Pat, and their two children were the very picture of the "perfect Christian couple." They sat together in church, and he told endearing little stories about their kids to illustrate his occasional sermons.

No one had a clue about the violence that went on behind the closed doors of their home.

One day Pat came to see me. There was a faint purple blotch on her left cheek, and an incredible weariness in her eyes. I guessed her problem before she even told me. "Vickie, I can't believe I'm going to tell you this . . ."

I prayed silently that she would find the courage to continue. Most battered women are so accustomed to hiding their husbands' behavior that they find it almost impossible to speak about it openly.

"My husband Darrell has a wonderful ministry. He has led so many kids to the Lord, and they all cling to his every word. He really is a wonderful man in so many ways. But . . ."

"Go ahead, Pat."

"He has a tendency to lose his temper, and . . ."

"Is he physically abusive?"

Pat looked at me in amazement. "How did you know?"

"Tell me about it, Pat."

Pat explained that Darrell had come from a violent, alcoholic family. His father had beaten his mother, and his mother had beaten her children.

One terrible night, her head bleeding and her face bruised, Pat had tried to confront him with his legacy of violence. Darrell had arrogantly responded, "Hey, that's just the way I am. I'm the head of this house, and I'll do what I want. If you'd do things my way, you wouldn't get into trouble. You're a lazy slob anyway."

Pat had been immediately apologetic. "I know, I know. I could try harder. But what about the kids? Why are you so hard on them?"

"Spare the rod and spoil the child," he'd laughed flippantly.

"They're just as lazy and undisciplined as you are. They need to be whipped into shape."

I listened sadly as Pat recounted her conversations with her husband. Unfortunately, this wasn't my first exposure to abuse within the church. Or my last. Such behavior is all too common, and it hides behind a clever mask—the misused word *submission*.

When faced with battered women, my answer is always the same: "You've got to bring it out into the open, Pat."

"What? But I can't! It will destroy our lives."

"Your husband is abusive, both verbally and physically. You can't continue to enable him in his behavior. It's wrong. And it's dangerous. Starting right now, you and I are going to work together on a strategy to discourage that behavior and help to heal the marriage."

Dangerous, Destructive Secrets

If physical violence is a pattern in your home, the worst thing you can do is to keep it a secret. When you hide your husband's mistreatment of you, you essentially give him permission to continue his bad behavior. Abusers hate exposure. And they know that some women keep their conduct a secret because they feel so ashamed.

Women who are abused almost always believe that it's their fault. The abuser has told them, "I did it because of the way you acted." Or, "If you hadn't said what you said, I wouldn't have done it." So who is getting the blame for it all? The one who is abused. On top of the punishment, she is also expected to take the responsibility. And unfortunately, abused women usually accept those accusations. They say to themselves, "Well, he's right. If I hadn't shot off my mouth, or if I'd kept the house clean, or if I had scrubbed the bathroom, it wouldn't have happened."

In fact, I have heard too many times about women who have gone to a pastor or counselor for help, and they've been asked, "What are you doing to provoke it? Quit doing it!" What does this imply? That men have the right to abuse women. If you go for help and are asked questions like that, find someone else to talk to—someone who will listen. What we have to do, with God's guidance and help, is bring about consequences that are so unpleasant that these men are motivated to stop their abuses.

Those consequences might entail reporting specific incidents to a pastor or elder—even to the police if necessary. A woman in church leadership should be able to provide you with good counsel. Unpleasant consequences might even mean that you have to leave home, taking your children with you. This is not done for the purpose of ending the marriage, but with the intention of healing it. Unless there is a realization of what life would be like without their wives and children, some men may never stop their abusive behavior.

And you'll need to be strong in your position. Suppose you say, "I want our marriage to be right, and I am not coming back unless we get counseling."

Your husband says, "Okay, I'll go to counseling." So you move right back in. What do you think will happen?

You need to see that your abusive spouse is seriously involved in counseling. He needs it, and so do you, so that ground rules can be established. And there has to be some system of accountability. Perhaps an older couple who have had a good marriage will be available to help lovingly.

Women often get locked into abusive situations for financial reasons. If they do leave and go somewhere with their children, who is going to support them? Most communities now have shelters and refuges. Extended family, such as parents, grandparents, or aunts and uncles, may be able to assist. And churches should be ready to refer women to homes that have been made available to abused women until something is done to heal the marriage.

Often an abusive man is frustrated inside. He may have been unsuccessfully looking for a job for six months. Many times a man like that has come out of an abusive home and is following the pattern he has observed since childhood. His mother "took it" so he figures his wife will take it. All of his frustrations come out on the one closest to him.

These men can find counsel in anonymous groups for abusers, which will help them work through their inappropriate behavior. The key to all of this is a sincere desire for change. And, unfortunately, most men won't see any reason to change if the victim of their abuse takes it silently.

Enough Is Enough

There is a time, in some situations, where someone needs to say, "Enough is enough," and "Stop it." There is no biblical support for the abuse of women and children to continue. For a man to dehumanize the woman who is his partner, his mate, and an equal with him before God is unconscionable. Within the church, particularly, it has gone on much too long.

Let me make a point here. You are not responsible for your husband's behavior. He has probably told you, "If you had done this, or if you hadn't done that, I wouldn't have hit you." No matter what you did or didn't do, a chronic abuser would find some reason to blame you for the bruises and injuries he gave you.

All of us can improve what we do. And your husband may not be entirely wrong in his assessment of your conduct. Nonetheless, his response is wrong. If you are doing things which you really should not do, of course you need to stop, but you must not accept this kind of behavior as normal. And you must not feel that God commands you to stay indefinitely in this situation.

There are times when it's necessary to exercise tough love. Sometimes a woman tells me that her husband is having an affair, and "It's not the first time, but he always tells me it won't happen again." I urge firm confrontation, even separation, to get his attention and convince him that she will not accept that lifestyle any longer. If he is willing to go for counseling and end his infidelity, the marriage may have a good chance of being restored. Women are usually so humiliated by infidelity that we must help them maintain their dignity and assign responsibility where it belongs.

High on my list of books for recommended reading is *Love Must Be Tough*. The author, James Dobson, maintains that we should not allow a person to continue in inappropriate behavior. He asserts that we are not supposed to be enablers, and when a spouse continues to provide "second chances," no ultimatum is issued.

Perhaps you've been taught to simply sit still and pray. But when the circumstances continue year in and year out, it's obvious that other parties have concluded they can get away with their wrongdoing. That's why Dobson suggests that wives give ultimatums to their husbands. When I counsel such women I often ask, "Do you want to go on all your life like this?"

"No, I really don't," is usually their response.

"Well, then, you are going to have to confront him. But the choice is yours."

When counseling, whatever you do, don't get locked into your position and say, "You can never divorce for any reason." An unfaithful mate has broken the marriage. That doesn't mean they have to divorce. Sometimes people will reconcile and find themselves with a stronger marriage than ever. But women who are the victims of persistent unfaithfulness need to know that they are biblically free to make a choice (Matt. 19:9).

Claire's husband was living in another city during the week, coming home only on some weekends. Finally, after six months or so, she came into my office and said, "Vickie, do you think he might be having an affair?"

I looked at her and said "Honey, of course he's having an affair! I can tell you right now that he is."

"Really? How can you be sure?"

I looked at Claire in amazement. Wouldn't you be a little suspicious if your out-of-town husband never told you where you could reach him at night, and the only place you could talk to him was in the office during the day?

Claire finally confronted him. Yes, indeed there was another woman. To make matters worse, her husband said he couldn't decide which one of them he wanted to stay with! Each weekend he would come home, and Claire would be there waiting for him, hoping against hope that he would stay. But after the weekend at home, he would invariably return to the other woman's arms.

Claire called me more than once saying, "Vickie, I'm so miserable. I just hate living like this!"

"I have real problems with what you're doing, Claire. You're allowing your husband to make a choice he doesn't have the right to make. He is married to you, and no one else. And unless you make that perfectly clear to him, he's going to carry on like this forever."

After several more months of agony, Claire finally called me on the phone and said "Okay, I am really getting mad!"

I said "Well good! It's about time! So what are you going to do about it?"

"I'm going to tell him that he either comes home to stay or I'm divorcing him."

She did so. And he moved back home. But believe me—as long as Claire's husband could have it both ways, he wasn't about to make a choice. They both have had to undergo serious counseling to restore their marriage.

Giving All You Can Give

Now don't consider all this an excuse to pack your bags every time your husband crosses his eyes at you! You know there is such a thing as conflict. Every marriage has it, and it is actually very healthy. Ruth Graham once said, "If Billy and I agreed on everything, one of us would be unnecessary." There needs to be communication, a way of working through issues without exploding. There needs to be self-control.

We must do everything we can to preserve our marriages. But we do not have to let things that are totally out of line continue indefinitely because we are told to "submit." Whatever it takes, do everything you can. Sometimes you may be wise to have a third-party mediator. Or find an older couple whom you admire—mature people who have worked through their own difficulties—and seek their involvement. You may need to seek professional help, especially when violence is a factor. But don't just place abusive or immoral behavior under the heading of "submission" and let it go on indefinitely. If you do, it will destroy you. It will wreck your marriage. It will devastate your children.

Sadly, hidden abuse and adultery are much more prevalent in the church than you ever could imagine. And as you reach out to other women, you'll eventually have someone approach you with those kinds of problems. Whatever you do, don't ever try to make a woman or child stay in a place where they are in danger of serious physical harm. Women have been killed because they hung on too long when they were told it was the right thing to do.

Some years ago there was a cover article in *Christianity Today* called "Wife Abuse, the Secret Crime in the Church." It is real and it is there, both in verbal and physical terms. If it is happening to you, don't be ashamed. Don't take all the blame. Get help. Get counseling. Get out if you must.

And as a concerned friend to someone in trouble, be compassionate. Don't just pat yourself on the back because it isn't happening to you. Instead, thank God for your own better circumstances and then open your arms in compassion, in counsel, in instruction, in prayer, and in firmness wherever this is happening.

God has given us His guidelines. Everything isn't always ideal, and there are no guaranteed happy endings. But as women helping women, we can help ease the pain, lift the burden, shield from danger, and leave the results to God.

7

Making a House a Home

*J*eanne gets up at 5:30 in the morning.

She chooses something chic to wear from her fabulous wardrobe, brushes her hair, and puts on her makeup.

She hurriedly dresses the baby and grabs his bag of bottles and food.

She kisses her husband Mark good-bye.

She drops off their son at day care.

She drives on the bumper-to-bumper expressway for forty minutes.

She arrives at her office promptly at 8:00 A.M.

Jeanne has an M.B.A. degree and works in a department-store buying office. Hers is a prestigious position in the upscale store, and the glamour of dealing with fashionable merchandise makes for an exciting career. Jeanne is proud of her position, but not of the small paycheck it brings her.

Retailing is a ripoff! she grumbles to herself every single payday.

Jeanne's schedule is hectic—she is either intensely involved on the phone or on the floor rearranging stock and keeping an eye on business. Most of the people she deals with are aggressive and determined, and by lunch hour she's drained. When there's time, Jeanne and her co-workers often eat out together at one of several better restaurants near the store. It's expensive, but the quiet environment seems worth the extra money.

After lunch Jeanne is hard at it again. She interacts with demanding store executives, competitive colleagues, disgruntled customers, and hardbitten manufacturers. By the time she's ready to go home, she's aching with exhaustion and dreading the commute.

During the day she often glances fondly at a desktop picture of her husband and son. Yet by the time she's reunited with the two of them in the evening, she's too irritable to enjoy their company. The baby needs her love. Mark needs her attention. But Jeanne needs nothing more than to be alone—relaxing or, better yet, sleeping.

The idea of a two-income family has driven Jeanne out of the house and into the marketplace. After lunches and month-end sales, she has precious little to show for her trouble. But she keeps her job for the sake of her self-esteem.

I don't want to be a boring housewife! she reminds herself when the going gets rough. *I'm way too smart for that!*

As we move toward the twenty-first century, our goal as women is not to become as much like men as possible. It is, however, to completely fulfill ourselves as the women God designed us to be. Sadly, our culture has blindfolded us, and we fail to see our vital, foundational, and far-reaching influence. It isn't always easy to convince women of their significance or to remind them of their immense responsibilities.

> As for you, son of man . . . my people come to you, as they usually do, and sit before you to listen to your words, but they do not put them into practice. With their mouths they express devotion, but their hearts are greedy for unjust gain. Indeed, to them you are nothing more than one who sings love songs with a beautiful voice and plays an instrument well, for they hear your words but they do not put them into practice.
>
> Ezekiel 33:30–32

That is quite an indictment, isn't it? God knows that sometimes we listen and everything sounds right to us, but we just don't allow truth to take root in our hearts. Caring for a home and children is God's best plan for a married woman's fulfillment. In many ways her domestic efforts are God's love song to the world. Yet working at home is almost becoming a lost art, particularly in America's urban and suburban areas.

Is It Really Worth It?

National statistics indicate that an increasing percentage of women with children are working either part or full time. And let me be quick to say that there is no alternative in some cases. Perhaps you are a single mother as the result of divorce or death. Maybe severe financial reverses have come upon your family. It could be that your husband hasn't been able to find a job and you've had to step in as a wage-earner.

However, like Jeanne in our story, some women are working because they have adopted the belief that being a wife and mother simply is not significant. They have been convinced that the only way to achieve personal fulfillment is to find a career outside the home. Unfortunately, for many of these women, the financial gains are too minimal to justify the amount of time and energy expended.

Suppose you are earning $18,000 a year. This amounts to $1,500 a month. If your income tax level is 15 percent, you'll pay $225 a month. Social Security, at 7.65 percent for the employee, comes to $115. If you just tithe 10 percent, you pay $150. If you travel ten miles a day (a conservative estimate) at 25 cents a mile, that's $50. All totaled that's $540, and you're left with $961.

If you can manage to buy lunch for $4 per day, you're paying $80 per month, even assuming you take your lunch once in a while. And since you're going to be too tired to cook some evenings, let's add another $80 per month for fast food. Extra clothes and cleaning expenses will amount to at least $50. And, of course, the big cost is for day care. If you have one child at $50 per week, you are paying $200 monthly. If you have two or more children, it obviously becomes more expensive.

So this comes out to an additional $410. By now, your expenses are $950, and I'm being very conservative in my calculations. (Besides, I think that the very fact that you have a little extra money in your pocket makes you spend more.) Subtracting $950 from your monthly income of $1,500 gives you a monthly balance of $550. Divide this by four weeks, and it comes to about $137.50 a week. You have to remember, too, that the additional income usually pushes you into a higher tax bracket.

Is that worth forty hours of hard work? Plus all the time it takes you to run back and forth?

Plus the housework that is always waiting for you?

Plus the terrible expenditure on your emotional reserves?

Sometimes we feel we are making a big contribution financially, but it really isn't as much as we think. Our energy would be better devoted to the most precious treasures we will ever possess—our husbands and our children.

A Queen's Domain

When you choose a career outside the home, there are going to be some consequences. There will be a lack of involvement in your children's lives. There will be physical exhaustion, which can erode your relationship with your husband. There will be a growing apart if your career takes you in one direction and his career takes him in another. There will be demands placed upon you in the marketplace that may not suit your emotional makeup or your personal needs. But perhaps the greatest loss of all is your removal from the place of power and influence God has given you in your home.

According to the Bible, homemaking is the God-given domain of womanly authority. It is not only our responsibility, but it is our place of influence and authority. I know that in some circles wifely subservience has been promoted and encouraged. I challenge it. I do not agree with it. And I think I have a strong biblical basis for my point of view.

I saw Anna before she saw me. She was making her way through the supermarket, her eyes fixed on her grocery list.

"Well, you're certainly well organized," I commented, trying to remember everything I needed to buy.

"Oh, it's not me, it's my husband," she smiled wanly. "He always makes a list for me before I go shopping."

"So he decides what you should cook?"

"Oh, yes. He decides every week what we're going to eat. Then he makes a list of all the ingredients."

"Does he help with the cooking?"

"No, he's not really much of a cook," Anna laughed. "He thinks cooking is 'women's work.' But he makes the list and then gives me the money for the food."

"How do you feel about that?"

"You mean about him making the list?"

"Yes—about him managing the menus and the grocery money."

Anna looked at me with a somewhat surprised expression on her face. "Oh, well, I think most Christians manage their homes that way, don't they? The man is supposed to be the head of the house, and the woman is supposed to help him."

With that, Anna checked her watch nervously. "It's great seeing you, but I've got to hurry. He's expecting me to be home in fifteen minutes, and he'll be upset if I'm late."

Of course it is going to be difficult to dislodge some men from their controlling positions. They may really want to believe that they have the right to be dictators and that women are nothing but underlings, required to obey orders. But God's intention is that you and your husband be partners—two people with one purpose who honor each other and respect each other's responsibilities and areas of expertise.

Paul wrote to Timothy,

> So I counsel younger widows to marry, to have children, to manage their homes and to give the enemy no opportunity for slander.
>
> 1 Timothy 5:14

As I pointed out in an earlier chapter, the Greek word translated "to manage their homes" literally means to be the "house-despot." That means the woman is totally in charge of the home. She is not to manage her husband, but she does have the right to make some decisions without him. She can choose to rearrange the furniture. She can decorate in a different color. She can purchase something as long as it's within the budget. She can sew different drapes. Of course, she should discuss with her husband his likes and dislikes and make their home a haven they can all enjoy. But she shouldn't have to beg and plead—that is foolishness.

The home is your area of creativity, an environment with which you can readily identify. A man has his work, you have your home. Respect yourself, and enjoy your responsibilities. Don't sit there helplessly wondering what to do!

Mary Helen was in absolute disarray. Her mascara was smeared across her magnolia-white cheeks, and her eyes were red from crying. "Oh, Vickie, what am I going to do? What am I going to do?"

I guessed correctly that Mary Helen was in her late fifties, a true Southern Belle with a lovely face and a gentle voice. She found me at a seminar, and before long she was telling me all about herself. "You know, my father was the most wonderful man. He did everything for me. He bought my clothes, bought my cars, gave me all the money I wanted. He even took my laundry to the cleaners and my dog to the vet."

"Your father sounds like an exceptional man, Mary Helen."

"Oh, he's dead now, you know. But George is just like him." She dabbed at her eyes.

"George?"

"George is my husband, or at least he was my husband. Last week he told me he's leaving me. It's such a nightmare! I'm nearly sixty years old, and I don't know how to do anything for myself!"

"You mean George has always taken care of you like your father did?"

"Oh, yes. George does everything. He handles the finances, the cars, the housekeeper, and the gardener. Trouble is, now I don't know how much money we have or what bank it's in. I don't even know what to do at a service station!"

"Haven't you wanted to know?"

"Why would I want to know?" Mary Helen began to cry in earnest. "I'm a woman! I always looked nice for him, I was always at his side, and believe me I was always there for him in the bedroom, too. Women aren't supposed to handle business. We're supposed to be pretty and not too smart. That's what my mother taught me."

"Why is George leaving you, Mary Helen?"

"Oh, a woman he works with has seduced him. That's the only thing I can figure out. This woman works with him every day on his projects, and they spend all sorts of time together. It's obviously just sex. What else would it be?"

If you think it's kind of cute and feminine to be dependent and helpless and dumb, think again. For one thing, men can become extremely bored with women like that. For another, you need to be prepared for any eventuality that may come your way. What if there's a death or a divorce? It's important for you to learn about the family finances. Find out about your money, how much there is and where it is. Get into the real world! It takes enormous skills to manage a home, far more than to be a secretary or even an executive.

Some Historic Models

Think about some of the women the Bible depicts. Remember the Shunammite in the Old Testament? She provided meals for the prophet Elisha. Then she went to her husband and said, "Let's build a room. Let's get him a table and a chair and lamp and a bed. Everything he needs."

Her husband said, "Fine." And they did it.

The amazing benefits and miraculous events this couple experienced because of the wife's generosity are indelibly printed on the pages of Hebrew history.

In the New Testament, Lydia said to Paul, "If you consider me a believer, come to my home." The early church could not have flourished without women opening their homes. For three hundred years there were no church buildings. What would have happened if those women had said, "I'm not up to entertaining today. I just don't feel like cooking!"

It was women who gave that fledgling church the warmth and the hospitality that allowed it to flourish. Romans 16 is filled with the names of women who worked hard for the gospel, who believed that their mission station was their home.

This is all possible because of the loving, sacrificial leadership that the husband is supposed to give to his family. And it continues on into voluntary submission, which is the wife's appropriate response to that leadership.

Your home should not be a cell block in which you are repressed and inhibited and ordered around. Instead it should be a greenhouse where you are allowed to flourish to your full potential, under your husband's protection, with his provisions and blessings. If we could get ourselves and our men to see that, it would change our lives and transform our families.

Most Christian women have heard, at one time or another, of "The Proverbs 31 Woman." To tell you the truth, this dear lady has always irritated me just a little. She is just about perfect, and my way of handling perfect people is usually to avoid them. I didn't want her to make me feel guilty, so I just decided that I wasn't going to read about her any more. However, when I finally studied her seriously, I was thrilled with what this very familiar passage was actually saying.

Before we read what the Bible says about this incredible "Wife of Noble Character," let's bear in mind that her failures are not mentioned—only her successes are recorded. The Word of God shares with us the sum total of her life: the intentions of her heart, her interaction with her husband and family, and her involvement with her community. The woman's everyday frustrations are not even discussed, but you can well imagine that she had her share.

I have a feeling that God looks at us with gentle eyes. Even in this very truthful tribute, He has overlooked all the negatives of the leading character, and painted a thoroughly positive portrait. I believe He does the same with us. He sees our hearts, recognizing our highest goals. He knows our built-in strengths and inborn weaknesses. He recalls the families we were raised in, the role models we had, and the experiences that scarred us emotionally. Our heavenly Father is well aware of our limitations.

Jesus Christ died for our sins, and God forgives them for His Son's sake. So when the books are opened on our lives we will be surprised at what God does not hold against us. If this woman is any example of God's way of viewing His people, we can trust Him to be very gracious to the rest of us.

A Woman to Be Reckoned With

Proverbs 31 describes the total life of this woman. She didn't do everything mentioned here every day—not even every month or year. There are seasons in our lives where we are able to do some things more than others. Furthermore, I think it's possible that this great lady may be a composite of many women. In any case, I don't think this passage is trying to tell us how busy we should be.

Instead, we should appreciate the vast scope of interests and activities open to women. If such an array of opportunities were available to a woman three thousand years ago, how much more can we expect to accomplish in today's complex world! We all have different capabilities and gifts, and I believe God wants us to use the abilities and interests He has given us individually, with an inner sense of freedom. Think of it this way: It gives Him pleasure when we become everything He has equipped us to be.

> A wife of noble character who can find?
>   She is worth far more than rubies.
> Her husband has full confidence in her
>   and lacks nothing of value.
> She brings him good, not harm,
>   all the days of her life.
>
> Proverbs 31:10–12

The word "noble" may be translated "virtuous" or "excellent" in your Bible. It is translated 245 times in the Old Testament. And most of the time it is translated "strong." It is used to describe God's strength. It is used to portray men who are dynamic and valiant. And here, it speaks of a woman's strength of character.

It depicts a woman who is loving, good, trustworthy, industrious, creative, skilled.

She is humble, discerning, organized, strong, dignified, compassionate, generous.

She is unselfish, unworried, peaceful, confident, intelligent, productive, joyful, wise, disciplined, enterprising, responsible, and authoritative.

This is nothing less than the picture of a woman under the control of the Holy Spirit. Clearly, this kind of noble character is available to every single one of us.

We also see that she is rare—one-in-a-million. And she is highly valued—worth far more than material wealth. This is the kind of wife we should instruct our sons to seek. This is the kind of woman we should train our daughters to be. We place such an emphasis today on outward appearance, peer conformity, pleasure, and entertainment. Let's remember to teach our children the joys of productivity, accomplishment, discipline, and hard work.

This woman's primary relationship is with her Lord. He has first place in her life. Consequently, her other relationships are in the right priority.

Meanwhile, her husband has full confidence in her. The two of them are a team—truly *one* in mutual respect, in goals for their family, and in responsibility. He trusts her totally because he knows that everything she does is for his good. This man can delegate responsibility and authority to his wife without fear that she will override him as head of the home. He will never become a hen-pecked husband—she will not grab the reins and run. His wife completes him—he lacks nothing. This husband has it all.

> She selects wool and flax
> and works with eager hands.
> She is like the merchant ships,
> bringing her food from afar.
> She gets up while it is still dark;
> she provides food for her family
> and portions for her servant girls.
> She considers a field and buys it;
> out of her earnings she plants a vineyard.
> She sets about her work vigorously;
> her arms are strong for her tasks.
> She sees that her trading is profitable,
> and her lamp does not go out at night.
> In her hand she holds the distaff
> and grasps the spindle with her fingers.
>
> Proverbs 31:13–19

Here is a wonderful home manager! This woman is an early

riser, such a necessity if we are going to get our day off to a right start. If we get up early enough, we can have a quiet time with the Lord, then plan our activities and get a head start in preparation.

This Proverbs 31 woman also knows how to prepare food. She plans menus, prepares nutritious meals, and delegates jobs to her servants. We know the meals are nutritious because she is physically healthy—strong and vigorous.

She is described as a merchant ship bringing her food from afar. She sells and buys wisely and brings the profits home—a good businesswoman. She is trustworthy with money, handling the family accounts with authority, freedom, and creativity.

This "noblewoman" invests in land, makes a profit and diversifies her crops. She is an eager, hard worker who delights in the fruit of her hands. There's a great sense of accomplishment in doing a job well, in producing, in success. This is not unspiritual. God has made us goal-seeking creatures (Eccles. 8:15).

In an agricultural society, the Proverbs 31 woman is fully knowledgeable and involved in every aspect of earning and managing the family income. She and her husband raise sheep, and she carefully chooses the best wool, weaving it into garments. They raise flax and she weaves it into linen. She designs and sews clothes for herself, her children, and her servants. She also sells the products she makes for extra money.

> She opens her arms to the poor
> and extends her hands to the needy.
> When it snows, she has no fear for her household;
> for all of them are clothed in scarlet.
> She makes coverings for her bed;
> she is clothed in fine linen and purple.
> Her husband is respected at the city gate,
> where he takes his seat among the elders of the land.
> She makes linen garments and sells them,
> and supplies the merchants with sashes.
> She is clothed with strength and dignity;

she can laugh at the days to come.
She speaks with wisdom,
    and faithful instruction is on her tongue.
She watches over the affairs of her household
    and does not eat the bread of idleness.

Proverbs 31:20–27

Busy as she is, this amazing lady makes herself and her bed attractive for her spouse. She keeps herself sexually inviting and available to him. And her influence on him is evident. A community leader, her husband is respected and honored. Her home management has given him the freedom to be involved in his community.

The woman in Proverbs 31 is always prepared for the next season. Her family is clothed in scarlet—high-quality, warm clothing for winter. She treats her servants as if they were part of her family and provides for them as well.

But her care for her family is not limited to material provision. She instructs them with wisdom and kindness. Since there is no other source of true wisdom, this implies that she knows God's Word and applies it to daily living. I'm sure this extends beyond her immediate family to friends who need counsel and encouragement.

She is deeply involved in her community. She cares for the needy and is compassionate and generous. Because so much charity has now become institutionalized, we can individually shrug off responsibility or just write a check. This woman was personally involved.

Can you imagine a woman with this much responsibility laughing at the future? Yet she does, because she knows she has done everything she possibly can to prepare her family for every eventuality. The rest is up to God. She trusts Him implicitly to supply whatever may become necessary to face unknown future possibilities—sickness, death, grief, loss, disability. This godly woman fears the Lord. She has joyfully placed the future in His hands.

> Her children arise and call her blessed;
>   her husband also, and he praises her:
> "Many women do noble things,
>   but you surpass them all."
> Charm is deceptive and beauty is fleeting;
>   but a woman who fears the Lord is to be praised.
> Give her the reward she has earned,
>   and let her works bring her praise at the city gate.
>
> Proverbs 31:28–31

As you contemplate this awesome role model, are you feeling a touch of despair, and perhaps even guilt? Please don't! Remember, Proverbs 31 overviews the entire life of a godly woman. She didn't do all of this at once. But she did use all the talents God gave her to the fullest, and that's really all any of us has to do. I am NOT responsible for the gifts someone else has. I must simply make the most of my own.

By the way, this woman was no doormat. She was not miserable, waiting to get out of the house to "find herself." She was queen of her home and family. And there was a wide range of activities open to her. In fact, there seems to have been no area of the culture that she did not influence, get involved with, or supervise. She participated in education, charity, business, manufacturing, sales, land investment, agriculture, ranching. You name it, she was involved.

She was confident of her ability. Her influence on her husband, children, household, and community speaks for itself. Her example to countless generations of women is immeasurable.

Just a Matter of Time

Believe it or not, every one of us can do the same things she did, as long as we have our priorities in order. We are not all called to do everything she did. But think about the scope of her activities. There was nothing withheld from her because she was a woman. She was free to do anything she wanted. All she needed was ability, desire, and opportunity.

You may be thinking that the role of homemaking in your life right now is actually the role of a prisoner. "I have these small children, and I can't do anything. I can't wait to be out and be free and prove myself in the marketplace." Well, this woman proved herself, but she did so working out of her home.

Homemaking is a legitimate career! This woman used all of her capacities joyfully, fearlessly, and creatively. She managed her home and gave it priority. Then, as time allowed, she expanded her activities and interests. You may not be able to imagine it now, but babies really do grow up, and toddlers eventually go to school. And all of a sudden you are going to have several hours of time that you haven't had before.

I remember when my youngest was finally in first grade and was gone from the house until two o'clock. For the first two or three weeks I didn't understand what was wrong. The days seemed so long! Then I realized that for the first time in twenty years, I had all those hours until 2:00 P.M. to myself. It was quite a shock. And before long, I was putting my "spare" time to good use.

Yes, it really happens! Time goes on and soon your children won't be completely dependent, requiring so much of your time. Please—don't be impatient.

As friends and mentors, let's encourage our young women to continue to develop themselves, even if their energies are presently being consumed by little children. These women were persons before they were mothers and persons before they were wives. A woman should never give up her personhood or her special interests. Any woman who stops sharpening her skills while she is mothering little children is making a big mistake. When those kids leave the nest, she will have no outside interest to continue to pursue. Young mothers must continue developing spiritually, intellectually, and socially.

Setting Proper Priorities

Married people have built-in priorities about which they really don't have much choice.

God must come first for us, whether we're married or single. We have foolish expectations when we count on our husbands to do for us what only God can do. That makes men into idols, and God certainly never intended that. God is rightfully jealous, and He won't allow any human relationship to take His place.

After God, the spouse comes next.

Then come the children.

Little children are so demanding and draining that it is very easy to inadvertently consider your husband after the children. I asked my husband not long ago, "What was the biggest adjustment you had to make as a father?"

"Realizing that I would not have all your attention," he replied after some thought.

It was the first time in thirty years that he had ever said it. But now I can remember little frictions that would arise, little arguments we'd have because I had to do something for the baby. I didn't understand it, but Fred was feeling the loss of something that he valued.

Putting your husband first requires a lot of sensitivity. You must give the child what he or she needs. And yet your husband must know that he has not been supplanted by some little helpless parasite!

After God, husband, and children, for a woman, her home comes next in priority.

Then you can reach out to others and, last but not least, to yourself.

If we reverse any of this we get ourselves into trouble. If we put other people before our families, we'll regret it. And if we put ourselves ahead of everybody else, we certainly are going to create problems.

The Single's Sphere of Influence

One wonderful thing about being single is the different set of priorities you are able to enjoy. Being unmarried can free you to serve the Lord wholeheartedly. Your first priority is the same—God. Next in priority is your job, and the next is other people. There is no spouse to consider, and you might not have children, either. Singles are relieved of a lot of the stresses and strains that married people have. They are freer to reach out to others in a way the married person cannot. They may have a ministry in your place of employment. Their integrity, excellence, and purity in relationships will support and confirm their testimony.

Don't look at yourself and think, *I don't have a lot to offer.* Instead, realize that there are other people out there in your sphere of influence who can benefit greatly from the gifts and talents God has given you. Married or single, if you get all wrapped up with your own needs and wants, unwilling to reach out to other people, you are missing some magnificent opportunities. I challenge you to look at your priorities. The ways you serve God and others are the only things that will count in eternity.

Scripture says that God has placed eternity in our hearts (Eccles. 3:11). Every one of us has a hunger to be remembered and a yearning to accomplish things that will last. For the married Christian woman, the greatest contribution she can make will begin in her home. It will be acted out with God's priorities in mind. And it will be accomplished because God has given her the means and the authority with which to do it!

It is my prayer that you and the women to whom you are reaching out will not just nod and say, "What a lovely idea. What interesting words!" Unlike Ezekiel's careless and insincere listeners, I hope you will hear God's Word. Listen to His love song. Believe it. Then put it into practice in your life— starting today!

8

A Mother and Her Children

*B*arbara had been looking forward to her high school reunion for months. She had been a popular teenager, and now that ten years had passed since graduation she yearned to see her school friends and catch up on their lives.

Josh, Barbara's husband, had suggested she buy herself some new clothes for the event, and she'd even had a manicure and pedicure so she'd feel especially attractive. Josh was out of town, but had encouraged her to go without him. "Get a baby sitter and have a great time," he said as he kissed her good-bye. "I just wish I could be there too."

I wonder what everyone is doing these days? Happily imagining the various careers and choices her classmates might have followed, she steered the car into the Sheraton parking lot impatiently. She could hardly wait to walk into the big hotel ballroom, pick up her name tag, and start visiting.

At first she was ecstatic, thrilled to see so many dear, familiar faces. But as the evening progressed, she experienced a growing sense of sadness. Of course everyone asked her, "And what kind of work are you doing?"

"I'm a homemaker and a mother," she replied. But every time she said it, she felt a little more embarrassed. Her best

friend Kate had become a lawyer. Sharon was a social worker.
Cheryl was teaching fifth grade.

"You're so smart, Barbara. I can't believe you're sitting
home all day doing nothing!" Ken had always been the class
clown, and he was still a tease.

"Well, I wouldn't say I'm doing *nothing*, Ken," she answered
with a smile, trying not to sound defensive. "I really do keep
pretty busy." Her mind flashed to the endless responsibilities
she faced at home. *If I'm doing nothing,* she thought to herself,
why am I always so tired?

"How many children do you have?" Kate seemed fascinated
with her family.

"Two boys and a girl," Barbara smiled, encouraged by her
friend's interest. "I'll show you their pictures."

"They're cute, Barb. They really are." Kate barely looked
at the beaming little faces before she handed the photos back
to her friend. "Jerry and I don't believe in having more than
one child. There are just too many people in the world."

"So do you and Jerry plan to have a child?"

"Oh, no," Kate laughed. "Not yet, anyway. And probably
not ever. I'm really kind of turned off with the family thing—
no offense, Barb." Kate patted Barbara's leg kindly. "Nothing
against you, but I think diapers and bottles and stuffed animals
are for girls who just can't do anything else. I'm gifted, and I
want to make the most of myself."

Tears stung Barbara's eyes. True, Kate had never been
known for her tact, but her words still hurt. Barbara glanced
down at her new dress. It suddenly looked frumpy to her,
and her carefully manicured nails seemed too short and too
pink. She glanced at her watch. It was only 8:30. *Maybe she's
right,* she mused. *Maybe I've missed the boat somewhere . . .*
She sat down alone and looked out at the laughing, happy
crowd.

Just then Sharon sat down next to her. "So tell me what
you've been up to, Kiddo!" She squeezed her old friend's hand
warmly.

Barbara smiled sheepishly. "Oh, nothing really. I'm just a housewife, you know."

Since the dawn of time women in every culture have identified themselves with homemaking and child rearing. Such an honorable vocation required no apology. However, in our contemporary western culture, humanistic philosophy has been incredibly successful in changing the way women view themselves and their worth, both in their homes and throughout society. Virtually every aspect of traditional female responsibility has been denigrated. This is particularly true of those responsibilities associated with domesticity.

James Dobson put it this way: "The term 'housewife' has become a pathetic symbol of exploitation, oppression and stupidity." I think it is an important undertaking for us to unearth the subtle influences this sort of thinking has had even within our more conservative Christian culture. Most of all, I think it is imperative that we take a clear-eyed look at mothering and see just what God thinks about its importance in our world.

Blessings from Above

Concepts like "Population Zero" and other global concerns have targeted childbirth and large families, not only in developing countries, but in North America. Their propaganda contradicts both Old and New Testament Scriptures, which promote the expansion of families.

God's command to reproduce was given to the first two people, and it never was rescinded. In fact, after the flood in Genesis 9:1, it was repeated again.

> Then God blessed Noah and his sons, saying to them, "Be fruitful and increase in number and fill the earth."

In 1 Timothy 5:14, Paul said, "So I counsel younger widows to marry, to have children, [and] to manage their homes."

Besides being a command, throughout Scripture the birth of children is always viewed as a blessing. It is never considered a curse.

> Sons are a heritage from the Lord,
>   children a reward from him.
> Like arrows in the hand of a warrior
>   are sons born in one's youth.
> Blessed is the man
>   whose quiver is full of them.
>
> Psalms 127:3–5

In Deuteronomy 28, God instructs His people about what their behavior should be in the Promised Land. And one of the indications of his approval was, "The Lord will grant you abundant prosperity—in the fruit of your womb." Having children was a specific sign of God's blessing and prosperity. On the other hand, throughout Scripture the inablility to have children was considered a reproach, a curse, a sign of disfavor, and a tragedy.

I do want to make a point here that is very important. Today, although children remain a blessing, infertility does not have the same theological significance. You can't say to an infertile woman, "Well, that's God's curse. You've done something wrong." All the promises for blessing in the Old Testament are in the context of Israel in the Land of Promise. We, in Christ, are under a different covenant.

I have a daughter who has problems with infertility. I was so encouraged when she said, "Mother, I believe that if God wants us to have children He will bring us those children when He is ready." She and her husband were willing to wait for God to choose when, if, and how they would have children. And He has given them a beautiful baby girl by adoption who is a wonderful blessing to our whole family.

I just want to reassure someone who may be feeling that her infertility is a curse from God. God has many reasons for sending trials and disappointments in our lives. Just look at Hannah in 1 Samuel 1–2. She became a deeply spiritual woman *because* of her barrenness. God needed a man to turn the nation of Israel back to God. So He started with a mother who would willingly give her son to serve God for life. Hannah was that mother, and she became the woman she was because of the disappointment and suffering she experienced. Her son Samuel led Israel all of his long life and then anointed her first two kings, Saul and David.

God's Fatherly Love

Besides being our "pride and joy," children benefit us in one very essential spiritual way. They model our relationship with God as a heavenly Father. In John 1:12 we are told that when we trust Jesus Christ as our Savior we become sons of God, children of God. The word in the Greek is "born ones" of God. In Psalms 103:13–14 we see how God uses human parenthood to convey His feelings toward us.

> As a father has compassion on his children,
>> so the Lord has compassion upon those who fear
>> Him;
> for He knows how we are formed;
>> he remembers that we are dust.

I find it much easier to come to an omnipotent, omniscient God knowing He is my heavenly Father than to an awesome, majestic God who is simply my Creator. Do you see the difference? God uses actual relationships that we have on earth to help us understand Him better.

In Matthew 7:11, Jesus compares earthly parents with our heavenly Father. He said in verse 11:

> If you, then, though you are evil, know how to give good gifts to your children, how much more will your Father in heaven give good gifts to those who ask him!

When we have children, they touch something in us that no one else is able to reach. They cut across an egocentricity, a basic self-centeredness, that is ingrained in all of us. Just think a minute how we willingly get up ten times a night, if necessary, to care for our babies. How we sacrifice our own comfort to meet the needs of these demanding, helpless little ones who are totally dependent on us. God also uses our love for our children to teach us about His unconditional love for us.

Have you ever had a child who strayed and broke your heart? Perhaps your children have disappointed you, rejected everything you stand for, and gone out on their own. Then they've returned to you. What did you do when they came back? Did you say, "I no longer want anything to do with you?" Or, with open arms, did you welcome them home? Of course you did.

My ability to forgive and love my children demonstrates how God's love for me never ends. If I, with all my capricious instability, can keep on loving children who are sometimes unworthy and ungrateful, how much more is God's love absolutely certain? There is something about having children that helps us understand the fatherhood of God in an incomparable way.

To Have or Not to Have?

Now here's a question worth considering: If children are a blessing from God and are so important to our understanding of Him, do we believers have the right to decide never to have children? Why would a couple make a decision like that?

I think that there are two basic reasons for choosing to remain childless. The first is, quite honestly, selfishness. "We both have careers. We won't be able to travel. We won't have time to do things together. We won't be able to afford our lifestyle."

And the other reason? I'm sure you've heard people say, "Why bring children into this terrible world?" That simply amounts to unbelief. In essence, it is a refusal to believe that God has the ability to keep His children for Himself, even in this depraved society. Believing that *does* take a lot of faith. And seeing it happen requires a lot of consistency, patience, and commitment on the part of the parents.

As we've noted before, there are three reasons for sexual intercourse, besides consummating the one-flesh relationship. They are reproduction, pleasure, and the prevention of immorality. You do not have the option to decide which reasons you like and which reasons you don't. You can't say, "Well, I love the pleasure, and I'm glad it prevents immorality, but I don't want children." That is really not an option that God has given you. You can't decide what to eliminate.

What about conception control—is that wrong for a believer? You'll notice I said "conception control." I am deliberately avoiding using the term "birth control," because some people bring abortion under that umbrella. We really want to control conception, not birth. And we need to ask ourselves, is that an option for a Christian?

There are two extremes with regard to this. There is one position stating that if you believe in the sovereignty of God then you will do nothing to prevent having children. Then there is the point of view which we just considered, opting for no children at all. But what about family planning?

Wise Family Planning

I read a book when I was first married written by Otto Piper, a theologian. He said something that really helped me. He suggested, "If the intent of the marriage is to have children ultimately, there is nothing wrong with planning." This is especially relevant when you have to regard the health of the mother, the health of the children, and the financial ramifications."

Personally, I think it's not a bad idea for a husband and wife to wait to start a family for the first couple of years of their marriage. This gives them ample time to fully enjoy each other before they have to be involved with the concerns of pregnancy, preparations for a baby, and childbirth.

Unfortunately, Fred and I had our first son just ten months after our wedding. It made our marital adjustments very difficult. All of a sudden I was transformed from a romantic partner into a sickly creature who was throwing up all day long. It was a miserable pregnancy, and it really did take the fun out of our relationship.

I know there are some books and teachers who maintain that we must trust God with our family planning because He is sovereign, and that is true. But I don't see any problems with taking advantage of advances in medical technology.

You are free to disagree, but I would like to say that if conception control is used, the method should be carefully considered. Of course the IUD is not really birth control, it's really a form of abortion because it prevents the implantation of the already-fertilized egg. Besides, IUDs have been largely discredited. Some have produced infections and sterility.

Many experts aren't convinced that "the pill" is safe. It can cause many side effects, especially if you have other health considerations. I have a problem from a health standpoint with a method that interrupts the normal activity of a woman's entire endocrine system.

Vasectomy and tubal ligation are very final and deserve extensive prayer before a decision is made.

One day a woman named Trish and I talked about this issue. She had been married before, and her ex-husband hadn't wanted children. She'd had some female surgery, and in the process had elected to have her tubes tied. Not many years later, her marriage dissolved.

"Now I'm married to the most wonderful man in the world," she couldn't help but smile as she talked about Tom. "But the trouble is, we really can't have children unless I go into the hospital for some fairly complicated surgery."

"Are you thinking about doing that?"

"Well, yes, I'm thinking about it. But it's expensive, and there's no guarantee it will work. I'm thirty-five, too, and I'm not sure whether it's too late for me."

"It's a difficult choice, Trish."

"It is. But sometimes I just sit and look at Tom and dream about 'our baby.' And I can't help but feel cheated. I know he feels the same way. I just wish I hadn't made such a final decision in the first place."

Although they are somewhat less dependable, the best choices for contraception are abstinence during certain times in a woman's cycle, or barrier or rhythm methods. If God overrules and gives you a child, then say, "Thank you, Lord." The fact is, we simply can't play God. And we can't be angry with Him if things don't quite go our way.

Our fifth child was unplanned. I was thirty-nine when David was born. In fact, I had already been thinking about how much freedom I was going to have when my four oldest were in school! But David has been such a joy and delight, it would be awful to think of life without him.

We just have to let God be God.

Guiding, Guarding, Giving Love

And what parental responsibilities do we have? The ones God has given us are not optional. We have the absolute obligation to provide for our children. This includes home, food, clothing, education, security, strength, and love. We need to remember that children are small, dependent, and helpless. They must have external strength to fall back on so they can relax and feel safe. They get that strength, almost in total, from their father and from their mother.

This requires your physical presence. A child's needs are not programmed to fit into your office hours. You can't say, "I'll meet your needs from four to five o'clock, but I'm busy before and after."

A child requires spiritual instruction. Christian parents must both model it and teach it. Please do not leave that to the Sunday school or the Christian school alone, no matter how qualified they seem to be. And, may I point out, the very first thing children need to learn is to honor their parents—and that means obey them. Ephesians 6:1 says, "Children, obey your parents in the Lord." Why is it important for us to teach our children to obey us? Because it also teaches them to obey God.

We are also to provide our sons and daughters with protection. It is not enough for us simply to watch them all the time. We have to prepare them to be on guard themselves. Teach them to look both ways when they cross the street. Teach them why knives and matches are deadly. And teach them that there are bad people who do terrible things to children. You've got to tell them that there are parts of their bodies that nobody should touch—nobody, including father, uncle, or brother. Tell them to tell you if anyone tries to do it.

In Dallas it is estimated that one out of six stepfathers and one out of forty fathers molest their daughters. That's not to mention all the offending brothers and uncles and friends and grandfathers. Sad to say, in some cases mothers actually molest their sons.

We need to give our boys and girls physical, emotional, and intellectual protection. That comes through instruction, and we have to be there for their spiritual instruction. Deuteronomy 4:9 says,

> Only be careful, and watch yourselves closely so that you do not forget the things your eyes have seen or let them slip from your heart as long as you live. Teach them to your children and to their children after them.

Reading on, in Deuteronomy 6:5–6,

> Love the Lord your God with all your heart and with all your soul and with all your strength. These commandments that I give you today are to be upon your hearts. Impress them on your children. Talk about them when you sit at home and when you walk along the road, when you lie down and when you get up.

When are we supposed to teach our children? During the day. Into the night. All the time. And that means that you have to be there.

We have a challenging job of disciplining them, too—a job for both parents. Please don't be the kind of mother who says to her kids, "You just wait 'til Daddy gets home!" They need to be disciplined on the spot, the minute they do something wrong. There has to be a connection between the discipline and the bad action. If you wait "til Daddy gets home" there won't be any logical association in their minds between their action and the consequences.

Proverbs 1:8 reminds us, "Listen, my son, to your father's instruction and do not forsake your mother's teaching." The two parents are equally important.

Some of us have been confused by today's humanistic philosophy. Current secular child-rearing literature has as its base the concept that children are born good and only their environment makes them bad. The Bible contradicts this view, stating that we are born with a sinful nature and that is why we do wrong things. Consider the following time-honored Proverbs. Obviously, God's Word is not suggesting or condoning child abuse, but is simply recommending firm discipline that children will understand.

> He who spares the rod hates his son,
>   but he who loves him is careful to discipline him.
>   Proverbs 13:24

> Discipline your son, for in that there is hope;
>   do not be a willing party to his death.
>   Proverbs 19:18

> Folly is bound up in the heart of a child,
>   but the rod of discipline will drive it far from him.
>   Proverbs 22:15

Do not withhold discipline from a child;
    if you punish him with the rod, he will not die.
Punish him with the rod
    and save his soul from death.

Proverbs 23:13–14

The rod of correction imparts wisdom,
    but a child left to himself disgraces his mother.

Proverbs 29:15

God's Gift of Discipline

Women with children at home are guardians of a future generation. Those boys and girls will become the business leaders, doctors, judges, missionaries, preachers, musicians, teachers, and political leaders of the future. The kind of people they will someday become is directly related to the commitment you make to them now. If you don't dedicate yourself to raising them, to giving them moral standards and Christian values, who will? Mothering is the single most significant thing most of us will ever do.

Being a good mother requires personal discipline. It also demands that we discipline our children wisely and consistently. God himself is our role model as a parent.

And you have forgotten that word of encouragement that addresses you as sons: "My son, do not make light of the Lord's discipline, and do not lose heart when he rebukes you, because the Lord disciplines those he loves, and he punishes everyone he accepts as a son."

Endure hardship as discipline; God is treating you as sons. For what son is not disciplined by his father? If you are not disciplined (and everyone undergoes discipline), then you are illegitimate children and not true sons. Moreover, we have all had human fathers who disciplined us and we respected them for it. How much more should we submit to the Father of our spirits and live! Our fathers disciplined us for a little while as they thought best; but God disciplines us for our good, that we may share in his holiness. No discipline seems pleasant at the time, but painful. Later on, however, it produces a harvest of righteousness and peace for those who have been trained by it.

Hebrews 12:5–11

God is raising us as His children the way we should raise our children. And yes, there is discipline involved. Discipline has both positive and negative aspects to it. There is instruction, correction, supervision, warning, admonition, rebuke, and infliction of punishment. All of those things are included in discipline.

But the word the writer uses for "trained" in verse 11 is an interesting one. It's the word from which we get gymnasium or gymnastics. The kind of discipline the author of Hebrews is talking about has to do with consistent exercise and training.

How are Olympic athletes trained? They work at their sport for hours and hours, every single day. One woman ice skater said on a recent television interview that she trains for eight hours a day. Hers is a continuing, constant effort to maintain and increase her skills. That is exactly what God is saying to us. We need to allow Him to train us, just as we need to train our children.

We can't allow our children to have everything they want, just as God doesn't always allow us to have everything we want. God disciplines us because He is our Father and we are His children. That gives Him the right to instruct us and train us and even chasten us.

But His discipline is a wonderful assurance. I once said to someone who was going through a very hard time, "Do you realize, this is proof that you are God's child? If you don't ever undergo discipline and instruction and correction and rebuking, it may be because you are *not* God's child. If you aren't at some time experiencing God's discipline, you are illegitimate."

We imperfect earthly parents have the responsibility to discipline our children, and, even though we make mistakes, our children are supposed to submit, love, and honor us anyway. How much more can we trust our heavenly Father, who never makes a mistake and disciplines only for our good?

God disciplines us because He is our Father. He does it for our good because it leads to holiness. No one ever became holy without effort. And no one ever became holy without discipline. The reason we discipline our children is so they will be good. We want them to grow up to have a good character. God is "exercising" us in His ways for exactly the same reason.

Discipline can be painful and unpleasant. It is a hardship. If the punishment you impose upon your children doesn't bring some discomfort, you are not disciplining them. It has to be painful because they must not want to face those consequences again. But I love what the Hebrews passage says at the end: *Discipline produces righteousness and peace for those who have been constantly exercised by it.* We are in a training program that will ultimately produce a people who are righteous and who experience peace.

In light of God's methods, we have to give our children freedom to make decisions. When your children come to you as they are getting older and say, "I want to do this and that," you will sit down with them and explain the alternatives and the consequences. Then you'll let them make their decisions, also allowing them to live with the aftermath. Sometimes that is going to be hard for you, but it is the only way they are going to learn to choose correctly.

Do you see the way God deals with us? God gives us the freedom to do what we want with our lives. He allows us to make choices—both good and bad ones—and subsequently allows us to reap the results.

One Highly Influential Career

Children need their parents' presence, time, attention, interest, strength, protection, discipline, and love. Meeting these needs is our privilege and a responsibility, not an interference or an interruption to some career outside the home.

Mothering demands more diverse skills than any other vocation imaginable. It is difficult to think of a more influential position in life than mothering, where a woman can influence following generations for either good or evil.

Perhaps you've been led to believe that children under five years old don't really need the careful nurturing and involvement of their mothers. Some psychologists maintain that boys and girls will become more independent if they are raised in child-care centers.

By now we have had a couple of decades of experimentation with this fallacy. Many experts in child development agree that nothing can replace the relationship between mother and child—it is essential to normal, healthy development. Feminine responsibilities are so vital to the next generation that the future of our nation actually depends on how our women view their roles as mothers. Children who are not bonded to their mothers can be irreparably damaged emotionally. It has been demonstrated by researchers that sociopathic behavior is sometimes the result of unhealthy family life in the early years and the absence of adult/child contact.

There sometimes have to be substitutes. But no one can fully replace a mother in a young child's life.

Now, this does not mean you can't take time out now and then. Believe me, an occasional break will save your sanity. You need that. We are talking about habitually leaving your children alone.

Dangers in Day Care

A recent *Reader's Digest* article reports that nearly half the mothers of preschool children are now employed. Parents are leaving their children at younger ages and for longer hours. Child care in large, state-licensed centers is seen by many as the wave of the future. This mass surrender of child-rearing responsibilities to nonrelatives marks a profound change in human history.

There is growing evidence that there are negative long-term emotional, intellectual, and cultural effects of leaving children in day care. Studies of children with a record of early nonparental care indicate that these children are far more aggressive than other children. They are often less willing to cooperate, and experience a higher degree of frustration. They are sometimes ill behaved, and can completely withdraw themselves socially. Many infants somehow feel that, because their mothers leave them every day, they are being rejected. This can cause them to detach themselves from her emotionally.

Research involving middle-class children in Dallas found that those who spent extensive time in day care were more uncooperative, less popular, and had poorer grades and study skills, and exhibited less self-esteem by third grade. The *Reader's Digest* article reports that Penelope Leach, a British psychologist and author of *Baby and Child*, insists that babies need individual care for at least two years.

It goes on to report that Burton L. White, who wrote *The First Three Years of Life*, a parent's guide for children, says, "I urge you not to delegate the primary care rearing tasks to any one else during your child's first three years of life. Babies form their first human attachment only once."

Day care has become a popular subject in our culture. Women talk about it as a feminist issue, while it is addressed by corporations as both an employment concern and a factor in productivity. The real question, of course, is, "What about the children? Is it good for them? Is it best for them?"

Please think about this summary from the *Reader's Digest* article ("Hard Truths About Day Care," October 1988):

What the very young want, and urgently need, child-development experts agree, is not education or socialization, but the affection and unhurried attention of their parents.

The truth is, a day-care worker is doing a job. If he or she manages simply to be a kind friend to the youngster and a reliable guardian of the child's safety, that is all anyone ought to expect. Giving the child the rest of what he needs—a self-image, a moral standard, life ambitions and a sense of permanent love—is too much to ask of anyone other than the parents.

Supermom Mythology

After Mom has worked all day, her hours at home are often strained, and she returns to her children drained and dispirited. Women have to recognize that they have just so much energy, and no more. It is impossible to expend your energy on a full-time career, meet the emotional needs of children, train and discipline them, keep up a household, and maintain a healthy, happy marriage all at the same time.

In *Time* magazine in 1987, there was a cover article called "Are Women Fed Up?" and this is a quote from it.

> This nation is filled with burned-out women. Partly because they are trying to pull off something that cannot be pulled off except on the Cosby show.

Women have been told they can have, even *ought to* have, husbands, children, and a career all perfectly managed. Yet even *Time* magazine says such an arrangement is a myth!

God Is on Your Side

You may have trained for a career, even earned graduate degrees. You may find it necessary to stay current with research and development in your field while your children are small so that you can return to the workplace later. There are ways you can accomplish that without neglecting your children. The same is true of helping to resolve family financial difficulties.

Ask God to help you. "Lord, my children are my primary responsibility. I want to give them everything they need. Show me how I can balance everything. Show me how I can keep up with my education. Show me how we can earn a little extra money. Show me how I can do it from my home."

Karla had successfully applied for an accounting position with a nearby company. She and Dave desperately needed the extra money she would earn—his sales commissions were dropping dramatically because of the recession. For days she had been poring over fashion catalogues, planning to expand her wardrobe frugally so she could reenter the work force in style. All things considered, she was excited about doing something new and different.

Then a visit to her doctor changed her plans drastically. "You're pregnant, Karla! Congratulations!"

"What? I can't be pregnant! You can't be serious!"

"No question about it, Karla. That certainly explains your 'flu symptoms,' doesn't it?"

Karla and Dave sat down together that evening, feeling some very mixed emotions. "Your job seemed like a godsend, but obviously there's no point in your starting it. I don't want to leave our baby in day care."

"Well, I hate the thought of it, too, but what are our alternatives? We're really struggling, Dave, and you're working much too hard." She couldn't help but notice the dark circles around his eyes.

Dave shook his head wearily. It was true—he was stressed and fatigued, working long hours as well as Saturdays. "I'm pretty well maxed out," he agreed. "I think we'd better pray about this, Sweetheart. God knows our need."

Dave and Karla held hands as they asked the Lord for a new course. They prayed that way for several days. Then one afternoon the phone rang, and a friend asked Karla if he could pay her to assist him with the accounting responsibilities for his small business. "I'll give you $250 a month if you'll help me out. I'm just no good at this stuff."

Just weeks later Karla had lunch with a friend whose husband was administrator of a local Christian school. When she learned that Karla was doing accounting work out of her home, she informed her husband. He hired Karla immediately to take over that very demanding part of his job.

Before the baby was even born, Karla had so many clients she couldn't take on any more. Now, years later, with her youngest child in school, she still chooses to work at home. "I can't afford not to! I make a lot more money at home than I can possibly make working for a corporation. God really knows what He's doing, doesn't He?"

If you are a single parent and must work to provide for your family, you can ask God to do something very special for you. Remember, God has committed Himself to be your husband. He will help you. He can show you a way to provide a strong, loving, Christian environment and influence for your children while you're away. And perhaps, with His guidance, like Karla you may find a way of earning your living from your home—many women have done this very successfully.

But I do want to encourage those of you who are staying home, devoting yourself to your children. Do you feel like you are wasting your time? Is your life boring? Ask God to give you joy in being a mother. And ask Him to give you an outreach so that you are not just locked into diapers and the kitchen. You don't have to spend all your time doing that! God can give you a ministry to others that will not take you away from your family.

Make sure your priorities are firm, and realize that you have God on your side. He will work with you so you can do what you are supposed to do. He will give you the strength and wisdom to do the job well. He will provide you with the diversity you need.

Whatever you do, place the same value on children that God places on them. They are a blessing above all other blessings. And the years when they are at home pass all too quickly. Look forward to the time when you can say, "I did my best for my children while they were home with me. Now I've got the time to pursue my own interests. And I can do so with peace of mind, knowing I did everything I could for them."

9

A Sister to the Suffering

A widow, Edith had developed rheumatoid arthritis when she was around forty years of age. Not many years before, she had been left with sole responsibility for her four children. When the doctor had first diagnosed her condition, he'd advised her to "get lots of rest." She'd smiled and nodded, well aware that following his direction was out of the question. She was working two jobs just to keep food on the table.

As years passed, Edith's hands grew twisted and claw-like. Simple tasks became exhausting. She fought an endless battle against debilitating pain. Although she had joint replacement surgeries for both hips and one knee, her condition continued to deteriorate, and eventually she had to take an early retirement from the work force.

Her friend Kathleen had often tried to discourage her from pursuing medical solutions for her illness. "You should pray, Edith. Pray and fast. If you had more faith in your heart, you'd be healed. I just saw a woman on Christian television yesterday who was miraculously healed from rheumatoid arthritis!"

Edith always listened carefully to Kathleen and never argued with her. The fact was, deep inside she felt guilty about her problem—somewhere along the way she'd read that rheumatoid diseases were caused by emotional problems. She often blamed herself for not handling life a little better. It didn't take much to convince her that she lacked sufficient faith for healing, even though she was extremely dependent on God.

When she was in her early seventies, Edith was faced with yet another surgery. "If you don't have your right knee replaced with a prosthetic, you're going to be unable to walk within a year's time." Her orthopedist had treated her for years, and she knew she could trust his judgment.

When Edith checked into the hospital, she was delighted to learn that her roommate was a Christian who loved to talk about the Lord. She was having surgery too, but professed a strong belief in faith healing. She was quick to point out that God could heal Edith's arthritis—if only she'd let Him.

"I've been asking Him for years to heal me," Edith explained, recalling Kathleen's countless admonitions. "And I honestly believe He can. But for reasons of His own, He just hasn't chosen to do so."

"Have you praised Him?" The woman looked at Edith suspiciously. "I mean *really* praised Him?"

Edith searched her soul. "Yes, I do praise Him—every day. I can't help but thank Him for my wonderful kids, and for the way He's always taken care of my needs. Do you know that, in spite of everything, we never missed a meal for lack of money, and . . ."

"Then it's sin!" the other patient interrupted. "There's unconfessed sin in your life. That's it! And I'll bet it's unforgiveness, isn't it? If you'll get rid of your sin, He'll heal you!"

Edith shook her head. She couldn't think of a soul she held anything against. She'd been through this course of thinking a thousand times before, and it always ended without resolution. *Wouldn't God reveal a sin to me if He wanted me to confess it?* she asked herself. Nevertheless, a sense of failure and hopelessness began to surround her.

Edith fought back tears. *Why do I have to be such a burden to everyone?* She closed her eyes, pretending to be asleep.

Meanwhile, the woman in the other bed looked at her and shrugged. She turned on a Christian television broadcast and began to hum along with a popular praise song. The woman was completely oblivious to Edith's deep heartache. Instead, she was feeling quite satisfied with herself for having "spoken the truth in love." It never occurred to her that she, too, was in a hospital awaiting surgery. She hadn't received divine healing either.

Facing Inevitable Pain

Sickness. Injury. Disease. Financial disaster. Death. Divorce. Suffering comes into all of our lives from time to time. We face it, work through it, and eventually emerge from it into better days. But particularly in the case of illness, we sometimes encounter additional pain brought on by well-meaning individuals who maintain simplistic views of health and prosperity.

Most all of us agree that God can do anything. God can heal. God can end suffering. God *does* heal and deliver and transform our difficult circumstances. Sometimes He uses human agencies in the process, and sometimes He doesn't.

In the case of physical ailments, we know that all healing is from God, but it's important for us to recognize that physical healing is not guaranteed by Christ's atonement. As our story illustrates, some Christians say, "If you are not trusting Christ to heal you, then your lack of faith is why you stay sick. In Isaiah 53:5, it says, 'by His wounds we are healed.' They would say that means we should always be physically healed."

Peter quotes that portion from Isaiah 53:5 giving it a different emphasis,

> He himself bore our sins in his body on the tree, so that we might die to sins and live for righteousness; by his wounds you have been healed.
>
> 1 Peter 2:24

Peter is talking about sin and salvation, and he is applying Isaiah's words spiritually. When we try to say that "by his wounds you have been healed" guarantees physical healing through the atonement, we narrow the scope of what Christ did on the cross. His redemption provides much more than just physical healing in this life. His redemption provides permanent healing by giving us a resurrection body that will never get sick and cannot die.

That doesn't mean that God won't heal or doesn't heal. He does. But the healing may come in eternity and not on this earth.

A Quest for Health and Wealth

Today the Christian church is permeated with a false gospel of prosperity. Proponents of this teaching assert that faith guarantees health and wealth. This is accompanied by the idea that difficulties, especially physical and financial problems, are the results of inadequate faith. It's vitally important for us to understand this kind of faulty reasoning so we can recognize it and reject it. Women will come to us in despair because they have been told this is biblical. We must be able to show them the truths from Scripture.

Most of the Scripture used to support this point of view is drawn from the Old Testament. In the Old Testament, Israel was promised that if she obeyed God and His covenant, she would be given physical and material blessings. In Deuteronomy, God said (in summary), "If you worship me and obey my covenant, I will bless you. I will bless you in your crops, your flocks, your family, everything. I will pour down blessing upon you. And all the world will know that there is a God in Israel. If you turn to idols, I will curse you; I will shut up the heavens. There will be no rain; therefore, there will be no crops. Your wives will miscarry; your flocks will miscarry. Instead of blessing there will be cursing; instead of fertility there will be death."

This was the condition for God's blessings given to govern Israelis who lived in the Promised Land. However, if you take God's Old Testament promise and carry it into the New Testament, what verses are there to support it? Where does it say in the New Testament that spiritual health guarantees physical health and material wealth?

In the New Testament we are promised spiritual blessings and spiritual fruitfulness. Wealth is not presented as a goal in the New Testament—we're not under an Old Testament economy. We are not the nation of Israel. We are not in "the land." And we are not under the old covenant. Yet some contemporary Christians have transferred these promises made to Israel as a nation and have applied them to the church.

Another error lies in the concept that all righteousness is rewarded and all unrighteousness is punished. The conclusion is, of course, that all suffering is punishment for sin. In short, if you are suffering it is supposedly because you are being punished for some sin.

Is it true that righteousness will be rewarded and that unrighteousness will be punished? Yes, ultimately, it is true. But God never promises total justice here on earth. This is a fallen world. That's why Psalm 73 is so comforting. The Psalmist couldn't understand why the wicked prospered and the righteous suffered until he "entered the sanctuary of God" (Ps. 73:17). Then he understood their final destiny. He then realized that his relationship with God was the only prosperity that mattered.

> Whom have I in heaven but thee?
>   And there is nothing upon earth that I desire besides
>   thee.
> My flesh and my heart may fail,
>   but God is the strength of my heart and my portion
>   for ever.
>
> Psalm 73:25–26 (RSV)

Who Is to Blame?

Now some suffering *is* the result of sin. And when that is the case, God will make it clear to us. But let's take a closer look at those things that we cannot figure out—things that really don't seem to have a logical cause. It's in these cases that the sufferer is sometimes bombarded with judgmental comments.

Even the disciples made that mistake. In John 9:2, they asked Jesus why a man was born blind. "Who sinned, this man or his parents?"

Jesus replied, "Neither one. He is blind so that God can be glorified." Was Jesus saying that those people were sinless? No, He was saying that they had not done anything that had brought on the man's blindness.

Job gives us a perfect example of affliction. Of God's purpose in pain. And of how *not* to treat a suffering person. Job's problems didn't stem from a lack of faith or a sin problem. He got into trouble because God was so proud of him!

Satan came before the Lord, and the Lord said to him,

> Have you considered my servant Job? There is no one on earth like him; he is blameless and upright, a man who fears God and shuns evil.
>
> Job 1:8

Satan challenged,

> Does Job fear God for nothing? . . . Have you not put a hedge around him and his household and everything he has? You have blessed the work of his hands, so that his flocks and herds are spread throughout the land. But stretch out your hand and strike everything he has, and he will surely curse you to your face.
>
> Job 1:9–11

Satan accused Job of worshiping God only for what he got

out of Him, and this brings to mind an interesting question: Why do we worship God? Is it because of what He gives us or because He is worthy of worship? God trusted His friend Job, so He gave Satan permission to test him. He said, "Very well, then. Everything he has is in your hands. But not on the man himself."

In a single day Job's wealth was swept away with no explanation. All of his children, all of his cattle, all of his servants, everything—gone.

Poor Job tore his robe, shaved his head, and said,

> Naked I came from my mother's womb, and naked I will depart. The Lord gave, and the Lord has taken away; may the name of the Lord be praised.
> In all this Job did not sin by charging God with wrongdoing.
>
> Job 1:21–22

Satan went back to God and said,

> "A man will give all he has for his own life. But stretch out your hands and strike his flesh and bones, and he will surely curse you to your face."
>
> Job 2:4

The Lord said, "Very well, then, he is in your hands; but you must spare his life." What does this tell us about Satan's power over us? It is limited by God.

Job again had no explanation for what was happening to him. Then his counselors came. For thirty-three chapters they "counseled" Job, repeating over and over their basic conclusion—*You are suffering because you are a sinner.*

Haven't we heard this somewhere before?

Job constantly said, "No, no, no! I haven't sinned!"

But his friends simply would not listen to him.

At the end of the story, God confronted Job's counselors. He said, "I am angry with you . . . because you have not spoken of me what is right, as my servant Job has" (Job 42:7).

God confirmed that Job was righteous. After informing Job's friends that they had misrepresented Him and maligned Job, He instructed Job to pray for them.

Finally, God restored Job. He gave him double everything he had lost—double sheep, double camels, double oxen, double donkeys. And he gave him seven sons and three daughters. Why didn't he double the children? Because the others were still alive in spirit, awaiting the resurrection of their bodies.

So here in the Old Testament we see a man who suffered very unjustly without explanation. Job was used for cosmic purposes, beyond his human understanding, in the great spiritual warfare that we all face every day. We learn from him that suffering happens for reasons beyond our comprehension. We learn that God is not pleased with judgmental "comforters." And we learn that God has the authority to give and to take, to withdraw and to restore His people's fortunes, according to His sovereign will.

Heroes and Heroines of Faith

In the New Testament we find similar evidence that suffering is not necessarily related to sin or faithlessness. In Hebrews 11 we read about great heroes and heroines of the faith. The author concludes the landmark chapter on faith by saying,

> And what more shall I say? I do not have time to tell about Gideon, Barak, Samson, Jephthah, David, Samuel and the prophets, who through faith conquered kingdoms, administered justice, and gained what was promised; who shut the mouths of lions, quenched the fury of the flames, and escaped the edge of the sword; whose weakness was turned to strength; and who became powerful in battle and routed foreign armies. Women received back their dead, raised to life again. Others were tortured and refused to be released, so they might gain a better

resurrection. Some faced jeers and flogging, while still others were chained and put in prison. They were stoned; they were sawed in two; they were put to death by the sword. They went about in sheepskins and goatskins, destitute, persecuted and mistreated—the world was not worthy of them. They wandered in deserts and mountains, and in caves and holes in the ground.

These were all commended for their faith, yet none of them received what had been promised.

Hebrews 11:32–39

Without exception, these individuals had trials. Some were delivered, and some were victorious. Others were not delivered, and some suffered and died. But they were *all* commended for their faith, both the winners and the losers. And none of them personally experienced what had been promised to God's people for future fulfillment.

Suppose you have a husband who is terminally ill and you pray and pray that the cancer will be healed, but it isn't. That does not mean that you did not have faith. Or that the church did not have faith. Or that there was unconfessed sin. It means that God's time came for your husband's life to end. And God is going to take care of you now that you don't have a husband. That's all. The outcome of our difficulties doesn't prove anything about our faith or personal righteousness.

If faith doesn't guarantee healing or prosperity, what does faith do? Why do we need it? Hebrews 11:6 says, "Without faith it is impossible to please God, because anyone who comes to him must believe that he exists and that he rewards those who earnestly seek him." Faith receives God's wholehearted approval and gets His attention. God isn't measuring and doling out hardships to you like somebody pulling wings off a fly. He is testing and deepening your faith.

How can we pray when difficult circumstances come into our lives and we just don't know how to handle them? We need to pray for God's will to be done and for God to be glorified. In doing so, we can't go wrong.

We can pray, "Lord I don't know why this has happened, but I want Your will more than I want anything. And I want You to shine out of this situation so that everyone who is witness will know that You have been glorified."

Then God is free to act.

You can apply this to anything. To the child who strayed. To the husband who cheated. To your separation from loved ones. To loneliness, sickness, or financial stress. To your past, or your future. To your own personality defects that keep you from really being free to serve God. In saying, "I want just Your will and Your glory," you are praying the way Jesus prayed. "Now, Father, be glorified in Me." Don't fail to remember that He prayed that prayer when He was on His way to the cross!

Something to Offer

What resources do we have as we confront suffering in our own lives or in the lives of others? Dr. Larry Crabb puts it well: "A relationship with Jesus Christ gives us indispensable and unique resources to substantially heal now and perfectly heal forever." You cannot find comfort or effectively minister to women unless you have that in mind. A knowledge of psychology will not suffice. *Whatever assistance you receive or provide in the face of suffering has to be based on faith in Christ.*

And, in reaching out to the suffering, you don't want to collect a lot of emotional cripples, dependent on you as their crutch. You want to help women and then turn them over to God. They need to establish dependence on Him, on His Word, and on His Spirit as they come to maturity. You should be there to help but not to become their "holy spirit."

Gary Collins writes in his book *How to Be a People Helper:*

> Suffering is a common thread in human experience. And in spite of theologies that might belie the facts. [As Keith Miller says,] "Our churches are filled with hurting people. Outwardly, they look contented and at peace. But inwardly they are crying

out for someone to love them, just as they are. Confused, frustrated, frightened and guilty, these individuals are often unable to communicate even within their own families."

Hurting people often view other churchgoers as a happy and contented group, unable to relate to human suffering. These people simply can't find the courage to own up to their own deep needs. Consequently our modern church is filled with many people who look pure and sound pure. But they are inwardly sick—sick of themselves and of their weaknesses, sick of their frustrations and sick of the unreality around them in the church.

Wanted: Real People

Do you agree or disagree? I have to say that there is a lot of truth in those statements. But is that what God really intended for His church to be like? If so, why does He choose terms that speak of unity, mutual caring, and mutual support to describe His people? He uses the word "body." The word "flock." The word "family." Human beings were never designed for isolation and independence. On the contrary, God created us with a need for companionship and mutual interdependence.

And yet our intensely independent American culture, which stresses our individual rights and freedoms, has robbed us of our responsibility and concern for others. And our mobility has made us rootless. It is difficult to sustain intensive friendships when forty million Americans move every year. These facts encourage shallow personal relationships. Consequently, there is a pervasive loneliness eating away at the deep inner core of millions of people, and many of them are sitting in churches.

Gary Collins goes on to say,

Several years ago a book appeared with a title *We the Lonely People*. The author observed that most of us want a greater sense of closeness but that we nevertheless spend our lives resisting this closeness. We want to have close intimate friends who know us, love us and are available to help in times of need, but we want other things more. Like privacy, mobility, convenience and the freedom to do our own thing.

Consequently, many us don't have that sense of community and family love that results in extending ourselves sacrificially to those that need help, need companionship or counsel.

Is there an answer? Yes. The Bible says,

> Two are better than one,
>> because they have a good return for their work:
> If one falls down,
>> his friend can help him up.
> But pity the man who falls
>> and has no one to help him up!
> Also, if two lie down together, they will keep warm.
>> But how can one keep warm alone?
> Though one may be overpowered,
>> two can defend themselves.
> A cord of three strands is not quickly broken.
>
> Ecclesiastes 4:9–12

We need relationships that get below the surface of "How are ya? Just fine!" Two are better than one because they can work together in a common effort with greater results than either of them could accomplish separately. Two are better than one because they can support each other when one is weaker. They can encourage and strengthen each other against adversity.

Maybe you're thinking, "I just depend on the Lord. I'm very mature spiritually, and I can handle my own problems." We are to depend on the Lord. But the Lord has chosen to use other people to counsel us, to encourage us, to support us. And He wants us to do the same for them.

Realize that our human bodies would starve to death if the food we took into our stomachs simply remained there. If the stomach did not digest the food and send the nutrients into the bloodstream to be distributed all over the body, we would die.

In the same way, the body of Christ will die emotionally and psychologically and will remain immature spiritually unless each part of the body does its work for the benefit of the whole. We all need to be continually developing new relationships and deepening present ones so they go beyond the surface.

We need to be transparent in our relationships with others so they can feel comfortable with us, not intimidated or put off by our seemingly "perfect" lives.

And we need to see those who are suffering through the eyes of Christ, caring for them with His compassion. Speaking to them with His wisdom. Reaching out to them with His helping, healing hands.

10

Clothed in Compassion

*J*ulie sat in my office, weeping softly. Finally the words began to come out, "If my friends knew what I've done, no one would even talk to me. I'm so ashamed of myself." She was so choked with emotion that her words were difficult to understand.

My heart ached for her. She was a sweet-faced girl, married, with a little boy. "Can you tell me what's wrong?" I inquired.

"It's so hard . . . okay. Here goes. I was engaged when I was nineteen and my fiance said that since we were almost married anyway why not have sex. We slept together, and I got pregnant and I had an abortion. I have not had a moment of peace for thirteen years. I feel like there is a wall between me and God, and I can't serve Him."

She just sat there weeping. "I had another child eighteen months ago, and I realized all over again how awful, how horrible the thing I did was. Vickie, I can't bear it."

Julie was so ashamed. She was also suffering from terrible self-esteem, as well as having an assortment of physical symptoms that required constant care. Her problem was affecting every aspect of her life. She had been to secular psychologists, but they had been of no help whatsoever.

I tried to help her examine her perspective on the problem. Essentially, she felt that she was unworthy to be used by God because her sin was so great—too great to be forgiven. She seemed to believe that she had to make up for the things she'd done wrong and that she deserved unhappiness.

Julie needed some teaching from the Word of God, which is what I proceeded to give her. First, I explained that the death of Christ was for *all* sins, and there was no sin He did not pay for. I pointed out that God had removed all her sin far from her, as far as the east is from the west (Ps. 103:12).

Then I said, "Do you realize that your baby is in heaven?"

She looked at me in astonishment. "Really?"

"Julie, do you remember David's great sin, when he took Bathsheba for himself and had her husband killed? As a punishment, God told David that the baby was going to die. David fasted and wept while the baby was sick, but after it died he resumed his normal activities. David said, 'While the child was still alive, I fasted and wept. I thought, Who knows? Maybe the Lord will be gracious and let the child live. But now that he is dead, why should I fast? Can I bring him back again? I will go to him but he will not return to me.' David wrote in Psalm 23 that he would dwell in the house of the Lord forever, and that's where he expected to find his baby. Julie, your child is in heaven waiting for you, too."

Hope seemed to flicker across Julie's face. She wiped her eyes.

I continued, "Do you believe that God will forgive and has forgiven and does forget?"

She nodded silently.

"Okay, Julie. Here's what I want you to do. For the very last time, confess the abortion to God and accept His forgiveness. You must accept His forgiveness with an act of your will!"

Julie bowed her head and prayed, "I confess the immorality; I confess the murder." She didn't say "abortion"; she said "murder." "I thank You that Christ died for that, and I accept Your forgiveness."

When she was finished, I said, "Now I am going to suggest something to you. What do you think about writing a letter to your baby?"

Julie smiled, "I'd love to do that."

"Just tell the baby everything you've been wanting to say. Once you've put it all on paper, tear it up. It's finished, Julie. Leave it behind you!"

She got up immediately and said, "I'm going out now and write that letter. You know, Vickie, this is the first time in thirteen years I've had peace. How can I thank you for your help and encouragement?"

Everyone Needs Encouragement

Larry Crabb said, "Encouragement is the kind of expression that makes someone want to be a better Christian, even when life is rough." Don't you long for an encouraging word now and then? I know I do. In fact, all people long to be encouraged. And when we consider this yearning in light of the Titus 2 command for women to minister to women, we can see how God planned for this need to be met. Women especially need other women to encourage them.

But what resources do we have for the encouragement of others? Many times I find that women lack confidence because they feel they aren't qualified to counsel someone else. Perhaps you have those feelings too. If so, I want to remind you of the greatest resource of all wisdom and loving counsel—the Lord Jesus Christ.

When we put our faith in Jesus Christ, He gives us eternal, spiritual life. In 2 Corinthians 5:17, we learn that by our faith in Christ we became a new creation—everything is new. And along with that new life come new privileges and new responsibilities.

Jesus is the great healer. He will abundantly heal today, and He promises perfect healing when we are finally in His presence. We can participate in His healing ministry by being instruments in His hands. Fortunately, as we learn from Paul's letter to the Christians at Colosse, He has supernaturally equipped us for the task.

Life, From God's Perspective

> Since, then, you have been raised with Christ, set your hearts on the things above, where Christ is seated at the right hand of God. Set your mind on things above, not on earthly things.
>
> Colossians 3:1–2

First of all, the Lord has given us *a new world-view*. We should perceive all of life from an eternal perspective. This entails a new value system and a new focus. The past is dead and we have a glorious future.

> For you have died, and your life is now hidden with Christ in God.
>
> Colossians 3:3

We also have *a new source of life*—Christ is now our life. His Holy Spirit dwells in us to produce in us the character of Jesus Christ.

> Do not lie to each other, since you have taken off your old self with its practices and have put on the new self, which is being renewed in knowledge in the image of its Creator.
>
> Colossians 3:9–10

This should result in *a new goal* for life. Instead of pleasing ourselves, our goal should be to please God.

Obviously this will involve *new choices*. God wants our will to cooperate with His will. He will not use us the way a master puppeteer manipulates a lifeless puppet. He wants mature sons and daughters who have gotten rid of old behavior patterns and have chosen, instead, obedience to His revealed truth—Holy Scripture. This appeal to the will is very important as we minister to others.

> Therefore, as God's chosen people, holy and dearly loved, clothe yourselves with compassion, kindness, humility, gentleness and patience. Bear with each other and forgive whatever grievances you may have against one another. Forgive as the Lord forgave you. And over all these virtues put on love, which binds them all together in perfect unity.
> Let the peace of Christ rule in your hearts, since as members of one body you were called to peace. And be thankful.
>
> Colossians 3:12–15

This passage describes a *new identity and unity*. We are God's chosen people. We are members of God's family. That's why these verses tell us how to act toward one another.

If we are going to minister to people, the first thing we need to communicate is that we genuinely care for them. Even though they understand that you won't compromise God's truth about right and wrong, it's important for them to realize that you'll still love them—no matter what. If you come into a relationship acting as if you have it all together and the other woman doesn't, your words and actions are going to have no effect upon her.

On the other hand, as we clothe ourselves with compassion, our spiritual garb will make us approachable, sympathetic, humble, grateful, discerning, and usable.

God wants us to let His peace be the umpire in all decisions. When women come to me for help in making a decision, unless they are faced with a clear moral choice, chances are I don't know what God's will is for them. So, when they ask, "Should I do it or shouldn't I?" I'll usually say to them, "Make the choice, and let God's peace be the umpire. If you have His peace, go ahead. If you don't have His peace, chances are you're on the wrong track."

God's Word for Heart, Soul, and Spirit

Let the word of Christ dwell in you richly as you teach and admonish one another with all wisdom, and as you sing psalms, hymns and spiritual songs with gratitude in your hearts to God. And whatever you do, whether in word or deed, do it all in the name of the Lord Jesus, giving thanks to God the Father through him.

Colossians 3:16–17

How do we minister to each other? "Let the word of Christ dwell in you richly." That is the command. The word *dwell* means "to be permanently at home." The word of Christ is to inhabit our character as part of our personality.

When you read "word of Christ," what does that mean to you? Does that refer only to the red letters in your Bible and the actual words Jesus said? No, the "word of Christ" means all of Scripture.

And how is God's Word going to dwell in you? By your familiarity with it. You should know some of it by memory.

Know its broad principles.

Know the meaning of the stories.

Know how to communicate its message of salvation.

Know how to exhort others with its message.

God's Word must dwell in you in abundance. And your knowledge of His Word will be disclosed in three ways—as you teach, as you admonish, and as you sing. The word "teach" means to give instruction and to involve the intellect.

The word "admonish" means to warn and to encourage and involves both the emotions and the will.

"Singing" expresses a joyful attitude of thankfulness and praise. Since these activities involve the intellect, the emotions, and the will, we are able to reach the total person.

God wants us to teach and admonish with every kind of wisdom—wisdom that is consistent with the Word of God. Sometimes you will read a Christian book and find ideas that are based on the Word of God. In fact those ideas may make biblical principles clearer. Do, however, be very careful about secular books. There is truth to be found in many of them, but sometimes it is mixed with error, and the reasoning is structured upon faulty foundational assertions. When we utilize secular material we have to be very discerning so we won't be misled.

Recognizing Legitimate Longings

As you encourage women, you will soon hear about their dreams, their aspirations, and their yearnings. Remember that there are two legitimate longings in all of our hearts—longings for security and for significance.

Unfortunately, instead of finding security and significance in God, people often seek for them in material goods, in sex, in power, and in relationships. And our goal, instead of pleasing God, becomes pleasing ourselves. Ultimately, we never find security and significance because we are looking for them in all the wrong places, using the wrong strategies.

A woman is likely to say to you, "I want to be married," or "I want to have companionship," or "I want to have a child."

Don't correct her by saying, "Well, you shouldn't be wanting those things." She is expressing legitimate longings. "Wrongness" only enters the picture if the woman is seeking them in her own way instead of waiting for God's provision and timing. When you can make that distinction for a person it is very helpful.

Masks of Perfection

We also need to realize that, at the bottom of our hearts, we are all afraid of relationships. We are afraid of reaching out to others because we dread their rejection. The core emotion is fear; the core threat is exposure which could lead to rejection. And so we hide behind masks. If we want to minister, however, we're going to have to admit that we're less than perfect ourselves.

Women want to know.

"Have *you* ever experienced anything like this? "

"Have you ever had any problems in *your* marriage?"

"Have you ever had a rebellious child?"

"Have you been tempted?"

"Have you ever failed to obey God?"

Please—don't hide behind a pious front, pretending you've never done anything wrong. Be transparent. You will have much more credibility if you admit that you've gone through some difficulties of your own. That is one of the reasons God allows us to confront problems, so that we can let others know how He has met our needs.

Goals and Desires

When women are sharing their hopes, dreams, and aspirations with you, remember that there is a big difference between a goal and a desire. I learned this wonderful lesson from Larry Crabb, and I hope you profit from it too. By arbitrary definition he calls a goal "anything we need to validate our personal worth." A goal is what gives our lives fulfillment, so if a goal validates you as a person, then it is necessary, and it can't be blocked by someone else. All of us must have some goal in life that gives us meaning and significance.

Now, just for the sake of definition, let's call the other good things we'd like to have in life "desires." A desire is not necessary for our personal fulfillment. And a desire can be blocked by someone else.

A good marriage is a desire, not a goal, because someone else can block it. The same is true of raising godly children. In either case, another person's will is involved, and that person is responsible for his (or her) choices. Pray that your desires will be met, but don't take upon yourself all the responsibility for the other person's fulfillment.

And as for goals? It's helpful to realize that there is only one goal in life that will really validate you. Only one goal will give you significance and the ability to go on no matter what is thrown at you. Do you know what it is?

> Finally, brothers, we instructed you how to live *in order* to please God, as in fact you are living. Now we ask you and urge you in the Lord Jesus to do this more and more.
>
> 1 Thessalonians 4:1
> (emphasis added)

Living to Please God

The only goal we need to be concerned with is the goal of pleasing God! And you can't imagine how comforting this is going to be for other women. Suppose a husband is straying. He is saying things to her like, "Well, I'm going to give it another three months and if you don't really straighten up, I am leaving."

Or, "I'm interested in someone else."

Or, worst of all, "I'm still trying to make a decision between you and her."

But suppose a woman simply says, "I am going to live to please God, and no one else." What kind of wife is she going to be? She will meet her husband's needs but not his outrageous demands. And he will not be able to keep her under his unreasonable control.

It is always the person we try to please who controls us. When the women I counsel are in the midst of marital problems, I try to focus them on the possibility that they may be living just to please their husbands.

Sadly, there are some men (not to mention some women, including mothers and mothers-in-law) who keep people under their power by never being pleased. They will never give their approval. In response we work harder, try harder, and yet constantly feel, "I am not worth anything because I never get a compliment. I never even get, 'That was a good meal, Honey,' or 'You're looking good today.'" Some people deliberately with-hold approval in order to retain control. Once we recognize that trait, we don't have to be slaves to their disapproval—it's their problem. Besides, our goal is to please God. We need to grasp this for ourselves, and then help others see it.

Seeing Life Through God's Eyes

Wisdom should include not only knowing God's Word, but also knowing how things work. We're supposed to be real-ists, not idealists. We live in a fallen world, not a fair world. There is injustice and we cannot always make everything work out right.

Suppose something tragic happens in life—a death, a ter-minal illness, a child straying, a divorce. Because of this event, emotions may be ravaged. What causes this emotional response, the event or our response to the event? Is any event so devas-tating that we can't go on living?

Let's learn to say, and teach others to say, "Everything that has come into my life has been sifted through the hands of my loving Father. He is going to use it in my life for good, and I know I can trust Him." Once we get hold of this faith, our emotions will eventually change. *When the will is set on trusting God, healthy feelings and actions will eventually fol-low.*

Always try to encourage individuals to express willingness for God to change their minds. Pray with them, and ask them to tell Him out loud, "Lord, I want You to bring my mind into agreement with Yours." This single step, if sincerely taken, marks the beginning of a new attitude.

If someone is suffering from grief, don't reprimand her say-ing, "Now look! You've got to feel better! It's wrong for you to be so miserable." Grief is normal and right—Jesus wept. If weep-ing over the death of a friend or a loved one was a sin, He would never have wept at Lazarus' tomb. However, sustained anger at God, because He has allowed suffering, goes well beyond the boundaries of normal grief.

Confronting Sin in Love

Sometimes, as you talk with a woman, you will see indications of sinful behavior in her life. It's important for you to be willing to point out those things. Don't jump in and say, "You did that wrong!" Instead, say, "How do you feel about the way you handled that?" Most women will be pretty honest. Then we can gently show them how their behavior differs from God's Word and His standards. And, by the way, it's necessary for us to treat believers and unbelievers differently when it comes to sin.

We need to remind believers of 1 John 1:9–2:1.

> If we confess our sins, he is faithful and just and will forgive us our sins and purify us from all unrighteousness. If we claim we have not sinned, we make him out to be a liar and his word has no place in our lives.
> My dear children, I write this to you so that you will not sin. But if anybody does sin, we have one who speaks to the Father in our defense—Jesus Christ, the Righteous One.

You've probably noticed that even when people confess their sins sometimes they still seem burdened with guilt. They can't forgive themselves. And, deep down inside, they really don't believe that God should forgive them either. Hebrews 9:14 tells us,

> How much more, then, will the blood of Christ, who through the eternal Spirit offered himself unblemished to God, cleanse our consciences from acts that lead to death, so that we may serve the living God!

You see, Christ not only died to pay for our sins, He died to cleanse our consciences.

Louise and I were walking together at a retreat. I could tell she had something weighing on her heart, so I'd suggested we take a stroll through the beautiful mountain scenery. After a few moments of small talk, she said, "I have to tell you something, Vickie. Ten years ago I committed adultery. I did it once and have never done it again. But I haven't had a moment's peace since."

"Does your husband know?"

"No, I've never told him. I couldn't tell anyone, because all my friends are pastors' wives or dedicated church people. Vickie, I'm so guilt ridden, so miserable."

"Do you ever intend to do it again?"

"No! Of course not—it is totally out of my life."

I had my Bible with me. "Let's sit down here for a minute," I said, turning to 1 John 1:9 and reading it to her.

"'If we confess our sins, he is faithful and just and will forgive our sins and purify us from all unrighteousness.' He can do this because Jesus Christ has paid the penalty. Have you confessed your sin to the Lord?"

"Oh yes, hundreds of times."

"Now I think, with me as your witness, you should confess to God for the last time, and then accept His forgiveness with an act of your will."

Louise confessed her immorality out loud, weeping as she spoke. She finally said, "Lord, I accept your forgiveness."

I then said, "Now listen, don't ever talk to God about this again, because He says He has removed it from you and forgotten it."

I turned in my Bible to Psalms 103:12 and read aloud, "'As far as the east is from the west, so far has he removed our transgressions from us.'"

I also showed her in Hebrews 7:12 that the Scripture says, "I will forgive their wickedness and will remember their sins no more."

"Now, Louise," I continued, "if God has taken away your sin and forgotten it, then He no longer holds you accountable."

Louise sighed and shook her head. "I guess I had to have a human being tell me I was forgiven. You know, Vickie, I never knew women could minister to women like this."

People everywhere suffer with guilt and confusion. Sometimes our guilt, like Louise's, is based on a sin for which we've failed to appropriate God's forgiveness. Other times we have false guilt. We feel guilty because a child has run off or a husband has strayed. We blame ourselves, even when we aren't at fault. It is helpful for us to teach women to recognize the other person's responsibility, and then to leave that circumstance between him and God.

And as for unbelievers? When we are faced with their sin, we need to give them the gospel! We have to show them that they are unable to change their behavior without God's indwelling Spirit. These people have to face up to the destructive effects of sin on their lives. Dealing with sin in the life of an unbeliever is a golden opportunity—their confrontation with personal unworthiness can bring them to the Savior.

Freedom from Fear

Linda asked to see me privately when I spoke at a retreat some time ago. She was obviously pregnant, and her face was streaked with tears. When I asked what was wrong she said, "My baby is due in two months and I'm afraid that my husband Bryan won't be there with me."

"Has he said he won't be there?"

"Not really, but his job requires a lot of traveling, and I'm just afraid he won't be able to make it."

I studied her face thoughtfully for a moment, sensing there was something more. "Is anything else bothering you?"

She looked away, took a deep breath and all but whispered, "I'm afraid there might be something wrong with the baby."

As gently as possible, I reassured Linda that every woman experiences that fear when she's pregnant. Then I asked her,

"What is the worst thing you can think of happening when your baby comes?"

The tears overflowed as she said, "Not having Bryan there, and having something wrong with the baby."

I took her hands in mine, looked directly into her eyes and said, "If those things happened—and I don't think they will—but if they did, do you think God is big enough to get you through them?"

I heard a very faint yes.

"Linda, fear of the future can make us miserable and take away our joy if we let our imaginations run riot. God wants you to act with your will, no matter what your emotions are. Psalm 53:6 gives us the answer: *When I am afraid I will trust in You.* Fear is an emotion. Trust in God is an act of the will. Are you willing to tell the Lord that you trust Him to take care of you and the baby, whether Bryan is there or not?"

Linda nodded her head.

"Why don't you tell that to the Lord right now?"

She bowed her head, tears streaming down her cheeks, and prayed very simply, "Lord, I don't want to be afraid anymore. I trust you to take care of me and the baby. I want Bryan there, but if he's not, I believe You will take me through it."

Then I prayed for her as well.

I received a birth announcement about two months later. On it was a little note:

"Jonathan is a perfectly healthy little baby. Bryan was here with me, praise the Lord. But I want you to know that I did not have a moment's fear since the day we prayed."

God gives us His peace when we give Him our fears. Not only is this a vital truth for our own walk with Him, but what a gift it is to share with the women we counsel.

The Priceless Gift of Friendship

As Alan McGinnis says in his book *The Friendship Factor*, "Life is to be fortified by many friendships. To love and be loved is the greatest happiness in all existence. People with no friends usually have a diminished capacity for sustaining any kind of love."

The Bible supports this need for friends. The Book of Proverbs says,

> A friend loves at all times,
>   and a brother is born for adversity.
>
>   Proverbs 17:17

> Wounds from a friend can be trusted,
>   but an enemy multiplies kisses.
>
>   Proverbs 27:6

> An honest answer
>   is like a kiss on the lips.
>
>   Proverbs 24:26

> As iron sharpens iron,
>   so one man sharpens another.
>
>   Proverbs 27:17

Friends are lovingly honest because they want the very best for the one they love. Have you ever tried to sharpen a knife? You take the file in one hand and the knife in the other and you start to scrape. Does it make a pretty sound? Not at all. But it depicts what we're supposed to do for each other. Refine the imperfections. Smooth the rough places. Sharpen the cutting edge. That's not always nice is it? And it's much safer to always be nice. Nevertheless, we need to sharpen each other, challenge each other to reach beyond where we are. That's what friends are supposed to do.

When my first son was small, he was a somewhat difficult child. And as a young and inexperienced mother, I was frustrated and short-tempered with him. I often found myself yelling at him and confronting his belligerence with my own strong-willed anger.

One day a friend was visiting our home, and she quietly observed my behavior during a couple of unpleasant incidents. "Vickie," she finally said, looking me straight in the eye, "you're handling him all wrong! You're completely out of control, and it's making him behave even worse."

He's my son, and I'll bring him up my way, I thought to myself, fuming inwardly. But somewhere deep in my heart I knew she was right.

Later on that evening, I was reading my Bible and came across Proverbs 18:21: "The tongue has the power of life and death . . ."

I sensed in my spirit that God was confirming my friend's words, difficult as they were to receive. My tongue would have the power of life and death over the spirit of my son and our future relationship. I had to change. Gradually, and over the course of weeks and months, I was able to change my reactions to my son. My friend's courageous words made a big difference in our home.

> Perfume and incense bring joy to the heart,
> and the pleasantness of one's friend springs from his
> earnest counsel.
> Do not forsake your friend.
>
> Proverbs 27:9–10

> The wise in heart are called discerning
> and pleasant words promote instruction.
>
> Proverbs 16:21

> A wise man's heart guides his mouth,
> and his lips promote instruction.
>
> Proverbs 16:23

> Pleasant words are a honeycomb,
> sweet to the soul and healing to the bones.
>
> Proverbs 16:23–24

I'm sure if you thought a little you could think of someone who did this for you. Someone who called and just said the right thing on a really bad day. Someone who encouraged you that you were looking wonderful. Someone who reminded you that you're a terrific mother, a great wife, or a wonderful friend. Pleasant words really are sweet to the soul and healing to the bones. Don't fail to give some away!

True friendship means love, loyalty, support, honesty, rebuke, instruction, counsel. There's a lot more involved here than just going to a movie and lunch together.

> The mouth of the righteous is a fountain of life,
> but violence overwhelms the mouth of the wicked.
>
> Proverbs 10:11

No Greater Love

Without a personal relationship with God through Jesus Christ there is no way for a friend to provide a godly perspective. That is the first thing we should offer those with whom we counsel. Without Christ there is no hope at all, and we have only our own human wisdom and strategies to fall back on.

We in God's family have so much more to offer.

We have His unchanging word.

We have the love He implants in our hearts for one another.

We have the powerful Holy Spirit dwelling in us, motivating and enabling us to do God's will.

So much of the suffering we encounter in our lives is entangled with the issue of human guilt. And secular psychology has no remedy for guilt. Many psychologists say, "You shouldn't feel guilty because there is no such thing as sin." Or they say, "Don't feel guilty about what you did. You have to take care of yourself."

But Christians have an antidote for guilt. Jesus Christ forgives our sins, and He cleanses our consciences from guilt when we trust Him as our Lord and Savior. We can present the women we counsel with God's love.

With His willingness to forgive.

With His plan for redemption.

With His provision for cleansing us from sin on a daily basis.

We don't have to give a theology lesson. We simply need to offer His love and grace to those who need it.

Maybe you are thinking, "No way! That's too much—that's just for somebody who has gone to Bible school or seminary." Well, that's not true. In fact, if we could reach people more quickly with God's wisdom and counsel and concern and prayer, some of their problems would never escalate to such critical stages.

Dr. Gary Collins is in charge of the psychology department at Trinity College. In his book *How to Be a People Helper* he asks this question, "Does friend-to-friend counseling work?" And here is his amazing answer. "When lay people with or without training were compared to professionals, it was discovered that the patients of lay counselors do as well as or better than the patients of professional counseling."

Dr. Larry Crabb agrees. I once heard him say, "Our obsession with professionalism prevents us from really ministering effectively to one another because we don't have the confidence in ourselves that we can do it."

That's not to say that there may not come a time when we must refer someone to a biblically committed professional counselor. But a large number of problems could be handled at a less critical level if we reached out caring hands a little sooner, a little more effectively.

Women all around us, in our communities, in our churches, and in our neighborhoods are crying out for friendships that are deep and life giving. Women need to be able to face their suffering in a loving and compassionate environment. As believers in Jesus Christ, we have that kind of friendship to offer—if we are willing to involve ourselves in the needs of others.

In John 15:13, Jesus said, "Greater love has no one than this, that he lay down his life for his friends." He did just that for you and me. He died for us while we were yet sinners—not friends, but enemies. And He has commissioned us to love each other, in the face of suffering and struggle, with that same kind of sacrificial love.

Keeping the Big Picture in Mind

As we've considered women in light of God's design for them, we've come to realize that no one can be as helpful to a woman as another woman. It's His best intention for us that we befriend one another, meeting each other's needs in areas that the men in our lives simply cannot address. Although the information we've shared hasn't been exhaustive, it specifically addresses a number of the subjects older women are to teach younger women. It can help provide us with a biblical basis for our own lives, and for those we counsel.

God intended that this world be perfect, and that our interpersonal relationships be totally satisfying. But life on planet Earth is sadly imperfect, scarred by selfishness and evil. Women have somehow lost their identities amidst all the distortion, not only in male-female relations, but also in their relationships with God. Only the redemption of humankind through Jesus Christ's death and resurrection can bring both men and women to wholeness and health.

Within marriages, homes, and families, the twisting of God's plan has been most tragically manifested. In areas of the very greatest intimacy, vulnerability, and need, sin has come in and robbed men and women of both pleasure and peace. Nothing short of God's grace can provide solutions for otherwise impossible situations.

As wives and mothers, as single women and widows, we have a great deal to give to one another. As we pass through our own temptations, trials, and triumphs, we gain depth of character and spiritual maturity. And we have comfort to offer

(2 Cor. 1:3–4). Because others are struggling, it is up to us to share what we've learned, what we have, what we hope for and what we believe in.

We have received precious insights, promises, and blessings from a loving heavenly Father. Like the loaves and fishes the little boy brought to Jesus, let's give our portion of understanding and comfort back to Him. He will bless it, show us how to distribute it, and guide us as we reach out to others—woman to woman, heart to heart.

Appendix

What Is Heart-to-Heart?

A program that has been successful in developing supportive friendships between older and younger women is one we call Heart-to-Heart. Titus 2:3–5 places the responsibility for teaching and discipling younger women upon mature, godly women. There are important reasons for this. First, women understand women. They have gone through the same experiences and felt the same emotions. Moreover, sympathetic listening and godly counsel often defuse tense situations before they escalate into crises.

Second, the immorality that is disqualifying Christian workers from the ministry would be avoided. Ninety percent of these situations start with men counseling women. To fill this role, spiritually mature women should have a biblical perspective of life, a sound working knowledge of the Scriptures, and a solid track record of godly conduct.

The experience, empathy, maturity, and spirituality of these women create an enormously powerful reservoir of untapped, God-given strength from which the church can benefit and should utilize. Women need it; Scripture commands it. The Heart-to-Heart program taps this reservoir.

This program can be initiated in any way that suits your church, consistent with its size and your culture. Informal gatherings can be used to kick off the program, enabling women to meet each other and quickly establish areas of common interest. They can choose their partners themselves, or a steering committee can match partners. The general women's meetings, Sunday school classes, and worship services should be used for recruiting participants. We give each woman a profile sheet to fill out to facilitate matching.

The following guidelines are suggested:

1. Make a one-year commitment to the relationship.

2. Contact each other once a week and meet at least once a month.

3. Pray for each other.

4. Do things together, whether it be Bible study, shopping, learning a new skill, or just going to lunch. Each set of partners is free to do what they want as long as they work on the relationship.

This ministry works. Some older women enjoy it so much that they are meeting with several younger women. And younger women love these friendships! They feel loved and have someone to call on for support and wisdom. Dr. James Dobson has often pointed out that women need socialization with other women. The isolation and loneliness women are feeling is not so much that the communication between men and women has broken down, but that the communication between *women and women* has broken down. Women need other women.

Furthermore, this ministry is primarily a ministry of encouragement. It is not necessarily a discipleship program, nor is this an in-depth counseling service, but rather a ministry which promotes friendship for support, counsel, and guidance.

This program can be started in any size church. Older women must be encouraged to accept this role because generally they have not recognized the value of their maturity and life experiences. These are their credentials for this relationship. The Heart-to-Heart program can become a source of healing, strength, and growth as spiritually mature women are given meaningful influence in the lives of other women. Women have unique needs that can be met only by women. In addition, as these critical responsibilities are delegated to these godly role models, the entire church will be blessed.

How to Start

Administration

The chairman of Heart-to-Heart is a Women's Ministries Board member, and her primary function is to oversee the operation of the Heart-to-Heart Ministry of senior and junior partners.

Responsibilities:

1. She shall select an assistant to help with administrative responsibilities.
   a. To help in matching senior/junior partners
   b. To help make re-matches when necessary
   c. To help coordinate and publicize social events

The chairman and assistant chairman use their knowledge of the women as well as the profile sheets to make matches. If possible, try to match women who are geographically close, and who have at least two interests or needs in common.

There must also be an appropriate age span between the partners. Generally, women under 30 are juniors; women 30–45 are either, and women 45 and over are seniors. Some women in their late twenties and thirties can become a senior to a very young woman, but also become a junior to an older woman. Most of all, pray that God's will be done in the matching process.

When a match is made, the senior partner initiates the first call to her junior, but from then on calling should be equal between the two. The chairman and assistant chairman should call their committee members monthly to find out how the matches are progressing. The chairman should also keep a file of profile sheets, brochures, entertainment records, suggestions, etc.

2. She shall select the senior and junior members for the Heart-to-Heart steering committee:
   a. To call the matched partners for follow-up and accountability
   b. To assist in preparing for coffees, teas, social events, and announcements

The steering committee consists of trustworthy junior and senior women who serve two-year terms. They are each given a list of matches which they are responsible to pray for and to call monthly. The juniors and seniors are called alternately through the year; therefore, each woman is called bi-monthly in order to see if she and her partner have met and if the relationship is going well. The partners' general comments are then recorded in the committee member's card file. The committee member may share ideas with a partner; however, any problem or confidentiality should be immediately referred to the chairman. If the problem is severe, the chairman should seek help from her authority within the women's ministries.

Publicity

1. Have a one-month sign-up period, beginning in September.
   a. Make announcements and provide information and sign-up tables throughout the church.
   b. Place announcements in the church bulletins and newsletters.
2. Host sign-up coffees.

a. Give one on a Saturday to accommodate women working outside the home (a nursery can be provided at church).

b. Coffees preferably should be held in a committee member's home, with committee members providing the food, juice, and coffee.

c. Provide name tags, profile sheets, and Heart-to-Heart brochures.

d. The chairman or her assistant should initiate a time of group sharing during which the concept and commitment of Heart-to-Heart is presented. The chairman should also encourage group interaction by presenting two or three self-revealing questions from which each chooses one to share with the group.

e. Ascertain if any women present wish to be matched together.

3. Give a Heart-to-Heart tea.

a. Have the tea in early spring.

b. Invite all the women of the church, but ask for reservations.

c. Have a qualified speaker give a message, book review, or personal testimony.

d. Ask a senior partner to share her experience in order to help urge others, especially seniors, to join the program.

e. Heart-to-Heart ministry should provide food, gourmet tea and coffee, flowers, music, name tags, brochures, etc.

4. Pass the word along! Encourage partners to tell others how wonderful the program is and how God has used it to minister to them.

Titus 2:4 Ministries, Inc.
P.O. Box 797566
Dallas, Texas 75379–7566

For more information on starting a Heart-to-Heart ministry in your church, look for my book *Women Mentoring Women: Ways to Start, Maintain, and Expand a Biblical Women's Ministry in the Local Church* at your local Chrisitan bookstore.